Leaving Dorian

A Memoir of Hope

Linda Dynel

Ella Bard Press Inc.
PO Box 1111
Lockport, NY 14095

ISBN 9798869685124

Linda Dynel

For everyone who has ever shared their story with me.
Your courage is a constant source of inspiration.
Keep moving forward.

Linda Dynel

The following is a memoir.

In that, I have been faithful to my memory, though I understand and acknowledge that individuals depicted in this writing may remember the events described herein very differently than I do. I strived to treat the very delicate subject matter with the utmost care and respect, and in no way intended to cause harm to any individual, agency or entity depicted. To that end, in many cases, the names of people and places have been changed in order to ensure privacy.

I am Krissy.

Linda Dynel

"Be subject to one another out of reverence for Christ. Wives, be subject to your husbands, as to the Lord. For the husband is the head of the wife as Christ is the head of the church, his body, and is himself its Savior. As the church is subject to Christ, so let wives also be subject in everything to their husbands. Husbands, love your wives, as Christ loved the church and gave himself up for her, that he might sanctify her, having cleansed her by the washing of water with the word, that he might present the church to himself in splendor, without spot or wrinkle or any such thing, that she might be holy and without blemish. Even so husbands should love their wives as their own bodies. He who loves his wife loves himself. For no man ever hates his own flesh, but nourishes and cherishes it, as Christ does the church, because we are members of his body."

Ephesians 5:21-30

Linda Dynel

Chapter 1

She was awake long before his foot made contact with her ribs.

"Get up, Pissy."

She had steeled herself for the blow, tightening her stomach muscles as his footfalls came nearer to where she lay on the couch. There was a time that she would have fought back, or at least sat up and tried to argue him into leaving her alone. Now, she merely prepared herself and let him do as he pleased. Minimizing the damage had become her main goal. Head down when he struck near her head with an open hand to minimize the chance of accidental facial bruising. Tense every muscle when he punched low with a closed fist to avoid having the wind knocked out of her. Go limp when he threw her to the ground and pinned her down because ligaments were easily torn and muscles severely pulled when her one hundred fifty-pound body resisted his three hundred eighty-pound mass. And no crying out, because the girls and the neighbors would hear.

She concentrated on making sure her eyes popped open with startled surprise at just the right moment and that her face reflected an adequate amount of pain, so that when she groaned softly it would sound to him as though he had really hurt her. If all three of those things did not happen in just the right way and in just the right sequence, he would realize that she was faking injury and would make damn sure that she had nothing to fake about.

She lowered her eyes and pulled the blankets nearer to her face as he walked out the front door. She listened for the familiar rub of the apartment building's exterior metal door against its weather swollen wooden frame, and she counted. One one hundred, two one hundred, three one hundred, four one hundred ... he was down the front steps and across the short front lawn heading toward their car that was parked in its space next to their building. Five one hundred, six one hundred, seven one hundred ... she slowly pushed back the pile of worn blankets and crept into the smaller of the two back bedrooms, the one that they were supposed to be sharing but that he slept in by himself. Eight one hundred, nine one hundred ... she leaned one hot cheek against the cool of the painted bedroom wall, trying not to disturb the closed window blind while she peeked around it. She could just see the chipped white paint of their rusty old Celica turning onto the side street. Ten one hundred ... and he was gone.

Krissy allowed herself to breathe.

In, out.

In, out.

Breathe.

Her hands were shaking and her heart was racing and all at once she wanted to jump up and down and cry and scream and holler out ... what? She didn't know. Instead, she gathered her clothes for the day and headed for the shower. She had a lot to do in the next two hours, and it all had to be done just right. If for some reason he came home while she was gathering what little she'd planned to take with her - if he saw garbage bags full of his daughter's clothes piled on the kitchen floor next to a bag of her own second hand things - she knew that the chances of her ever getting out of that apartment again were slim at best. And then what would happen to her girls? She brushed her teeth and tried to will away the fear that was closing her throat and making her want to throw up.

She looked at herself in the bathroom mirror after rinsing and spitting and knew that the voice that she'd heard only a week before was true and right and good. The voice had spoken to her with undeniable clarity and purpose as she was going about her daily routine one sunny afternoon, gathering laundry and thinking about what she was going to make for dinner. It had said, "I do not want you living like this." The voice was real. Like a man she knew but then again didn't; a man that was standing just above and behind her. His voice was familiar and stern and definitive.

That had changed everything. Suddenly Krissy knew what she had to do; she had to take Anna and Grace and run away. She didn't know how she was going to do it but she knew that the voice was bigger than her, and that the message was bigger than the words, and that it was time. All of her praying for an answer and praying for a solution and praying for a cure to the ailment that afflicted her little family had been given to her in that one tidy directive. And though trying to figure out what a life lived out from under Dorian's control had at first seemed impossible, over the past week Krissy had forced herself to try and imagine it. To try and imagine peace.

As she stepped into the shower, goosebumps rose to cover all of her pale and damaged body. She deliberately avoided looking at the sickening array of colors that made up the dozen or so old and new bruises that were sprinkled over her legs, torso and upper arms. They all sang a song of failure and weakness and shame. And though she'd decided that it might be helpful to give them a good once over, if for nothing else than strength of purpose, when it came time to open her eyes and look at some of what Dorian had done to her and would surely continue to do to her, Krissy simply couldn't manage. Instead, she closed her eyes and breathed in deeply and tried to focus on the time frame. Her brother Spence had told her that he would be arriving at nine o'clock sharp, and had assured her that they'd be out by nine-thirty.

Out by nine-thirty.

Out.

She focused on the numbers and that one tiny word and tried to purposefully relax so that her hands might stop shaking. She was actually going to do it. She was going to leave Dorian.

Chapter 2

Krissy had met Dorian after answering the personal ad he'd listed in a local newspaper. She'd only recently moved out of the apartment that she'd shared with her college boyfriend and back into the grungy, two-story house that her mother had moved her and her younger brother into a few years before. It was a rental, and its worn, uncarpeted floors, leaky plumbing and drafty windows were just like all the other dozen or so run-down places the three of them had lived in.

Once Krissy graduated high school and had her acceptance letter and room assignment for the University of Buffalo in hand, she'd sworn that she would never again live under the same roof as her mother. Lenore appeared to have shared Krissy's sentiment, as she couldn't leave fast enough that bright August day that she and Spence had delivered Krissy to the brick walled fifteen by fifteen-foot dorm room that the excited but apprehensive eighteen-year-old had accepted plenty of financial aid in order to be able to afford. Lenore didn't even give Krissy a hug; just lit a cigarette as she stepped back out into the crowded hallway and waved goodbye with a, 'have fun' and a smile.

Unfortunately, it quickly became apparent to Krissy that dorm life was vastly different than what she'd anticipated; it was noisy and crowded and the lack of privacy wore on her quickly. Krissy had been 'born an adult', that's what Lenore had been fond of saying when she was home and sober and awake enough to say anything. And that had been fine when Krissy had lived at home; a nine-year old that could get her younger brother off the school bus in the afternoon, make dinner for them both, watch over him while he finished his homework, and got ready for bed was more than a welcome convenience for a newly single mom who was either sleeping or partying when she wasn't at work. But campus life was geared toward kids who were trying to break free of their parental bonds, and after years of raising her brother and looking after herself and being treated more like her mother's therapist than her daughter, Krissy didn't have much use for chaos. More than anything, she wanted stability.

Had that mature, clear headed, focused attitude lasted more than a couple of weeks, Krissy might have stood a fair chance of actually accomplishing something that first semester at school. Instead, by the end of September, Krissy was hot and heavy with the boy that lived in the dorm room next to hers. Having never learned moderation, discretion or self-respect, she dove headlong into partying all night, sleeping all day and carrying on with that Boy Next Door. When the notice that came with her second semester grades proved beyond a shadow of a doubt that what her roommate had told her was true - that if you didn't keep your grades up you could lose your financial aid - Krissy was left to figure out not only how she was going to pay for college, but also where she was going to live if she didn't attend. Moving back in with her mother was not an option she wanted to have to entertain.

The Boy Next Door was flunking out as well, and it wasn't long before his father was on the phone letting him know that there would be no more throwing good money at bad. Soon push came to shove and the two realized that they might never see each other again if something didn't give. They decided their only option was to move in together. They ditched the dorms and rented a cheap basement apartment just off campus. Mildew grew up the walls in the bedroom and the windows were small and sunless no matter the weather, but it was mostly clean and the neighbors were quiet and it gave Krissy a sense of peace to have a space that was all her own.

The importance of completing her education faded away under the more imminent necessity of meeting the monthly bills. By the middle of October, Krissy had dropped out of school and had taken a job working in the kitchen of a nursing home. She paid the rent and bought the groceries and did the laundry and cleaned their tiny apartment all while the Boy Next Door quit job after job.

It wasn't long before all pretense was gone that the Boy Next Door was going to do anything all day other than sit at his computer, smoke cigarettes and drink pot after pot of coffee. Krissy worked and he played his video games and they lived like that for a couple of years until he started talking about wanting to try a little bondage in the bedroom. Krissy also started to suspect that he was wearing her clothes when she was at work. After he pushed her hard one morning after she'd accidentally burned his arm with a hot curling iron, Krissy started to think that maybe it was time to move on. This time, moving back in with her mother was her only option, and Krissy grudgingly accepted that fact. It would be the one and only time she would give in and go home, she promised herself. Within weeks of moving back in with Lenore, who by this time had not only been diagnosed with a variety of psychological ailments but was also suffering through a particularly nasty menopause with the help of psychotropic drugs and a bottle of scotch she kept hidden in her bedroom closet, Krissy was lonely and miserable and looking for a distraction from her dead-end job and what appeared to be shaping up to be her dead-end life.

Since her mother had sold her childhood bedroom set within months of her departure to school, Krissy ended up having to sleep on the floor on a mattress that her mother's hoarder-boyfriend had salvaged from a vintage camper. Her former bedroom was stacked top to bottom with boxes of his mess: car parts and fishing poles and dirty stuffed animals and all sorts of other oddities that the somber old man had garbage-picked over the years since Krissy had moved out.

She'd had to bring her small black cat, Mickey, home with her as well. At night she would lay awake and stroke the cat's short, rough fur and stare at the precariously stacked piles that loomed all around her and wonder how she was ever going to escape such madness. Then while perusing the help wanted ads in the newspaper one evening after a particularly tedious day at work, she came across the personals. It was mid-August, and one sure sign that summer was drawing to a close was that advertisements for the county fair had started appearing in the newspapers and on TV.

Krissy had been to the fair once when she was a little kid, with her dad. It was on one of the rare occasions that Buzby, the man whom Lenore had categorically dismissed from her children's lives after an acrid and painful divorce, had come to town to visit. Her dad had held her hand and joked with her while they'd walked the fairgrounds, the two of them trailing slowly behind little Spence as he ran off a belly of cotton candy and soda. Krissy could not remember a time in her whole life that she'd felt more loved.

She'd also been to the fair a couple of times since, with high school friends and boyfriends. The magical glow of the lights on the rides, the oily, sweet smell of kettle corn and the noise of the carnies shouting from their booths had been a welcome respite, if only for an evening, from the chaos and uncertainty that she lived with at home every day.

The fair always set up in Hamburg, a town just south of Buffalo. The drive was easily thirty minutes from Lenore's house, and since she had no car of her own and none of her girlfriends wanted to go, not even after she'd offered to pitch in for gas, Krissy had no idea how she was going to get there.

Once she finished looking at the help wanted ads, Krissy flipped to the back page of the paper where she'd noticed the section marked "Personal Ads". She paused a moment. Maybe, she thought, she could try and round herself up a date for the fair. Why not? There were plenty of ads to choose from. And while she was no beauty queen, she was cute enough and reasonably bright and loved to talk. She was sure that somewhere in the thirty or so ads labeled "Men Seeking Women" there would be at least one nice guy in her age range that she might be able to plan a date with. Yes, a first date to the fair seemed reasonable and innocent enough, and it would be a full day away from the suffocating intensity of her mother's four walls.

Since the day she'd moved back, Krissy had found herself thinking almost constantly about escaping, and had been squirreling away as much of her meager paychecks as she could every week in hopes of having enough money saved up by Halloween to pay first month's rent and security on a place of her own. She didn't know how much longer she was going to be able to manage living under the same roof as Lenore. Though she knew it wasn't possible, considering how awful she'd felt each and every day since she'd moved back in, sometimes Krissy wondered if crazy wasn't contagious.

Linda Dynel

Chapter 3

Krissy hadn't washed her hair; she'd simply tucked it up into a shower cap and brushed it out once she was dressed. Her hair was long; it hung down to her waist and was all one length except for her bangs. Both of her girls had hair that hung to their waists, too. Dorian liked that. He wanted his girls to look like girls; none of that short, butch-dyke stuff on his wife or daughters. But no fancy hair styles, either. Who the hell was Krissy trying to look good for, anyway, he'd rail as he paced back and forth outside the bathroom as she was doing her hair for work. He liked her hair long and girly. She wasn't thinking about cutting it, was she?

She did have that one friend back in high school that was a dyke. Maybe Krissy thought about her sometimes and wanted to go all butch-dyke, too? Was that right, he'd needle her relentlessly as she put on her makeup: Was she? Was she? Was she? She never wanted relations with him anymore. Maybe she was thinking about that old high school 'friend', he'd rant, raising his short, fat fingers into air quotes. Maybe she was thinking about finding that old 'friend' again and doing a little coochie-dancing. You dreaming about coochie-dancing with that old dyke friend of yours, Pissy? That's a sin, he'd growl loudly. God hates homos; you know that, right, Pissy? She *had* been a dyke in high school, hadn't she, he'd hiss at her, trying to provoke her into a fight as she worked her thick hair into the long, tidy French braid she wore for her job as a restaurant manager. Dorian would go on and on, barking and cackling at her while the girls played on the plastic outdoor climber that he'd set up in the middle of their almost empty living room.

Krissy had decided the evening before that she was going to try and keep some of the morning as normal as possible. She'd wake the girls up and put them in front of the television to watch a religious kid's video, then prayers before breakfast, just like always. But then she'd let them watch their favorite secular video while they ate. Once they were done with breakfast, she'd dress them and brush their teeth, same as always, but then they'd get to continue watching TV. There would be no homeschool that morning.

Even before Anna had been born, Dorian had insisted that any children that he and Krissy had would be homeschooled. No child of his was going to go to public school, or worse yet, parochial school. According to Dorian, the public school system was corrupt from the inside out, funded by America's immoral Liberal government for the sole purpose of corrupting all of God's Little Children. He didn't want his children exposed to liberal teachers who would fill their heads with anti-Catholic, Masonic, Pro-Choice rhetoric. And since parochial school could not be considered an option either, what with the Church's acceptance of public and governmental funding, as well as the fact that he was sure that most nuns were lesbians and that the vast majority of priests could not be trusted to keep their hands off little kids, the only option for their children would be homeschool.

Krissy put on a religious video, then got the girls up like she did every morning. She watched them waddle and stumble around the brightly colored play gym and collapse again with their stuffed animals onto the second-hand couch that sat against the living room's far wall. She toasted waffles and microwaved sausage links and tried to breathe.

She was taking her daughters away from their father.

They were only three and four years old, though as little as they were, Dorian would tell them over and over again that he stood in the place of God the Father for them. He would tell them that he was the Head of the Household and the Boss of the House. He told them that he would lead them to Heaven. He would use his Daddy Voice while they were sitting on his lap and he was reading to them from their Children's Bibles. He tried to make sure that they understood that they were never to question his judgment and never, ever, to do anything other than just exactly what he told them. He promised them that if they listened to Daddy, God the Father would always think that they were good girls. Good girls always went to Heaven, and that's where he wanted them to go someday; to Heaven.

Krissy turned off the TV and popped the video out of the VCR, then sat their small plastic breakfast plates on the table. She helped Grace into her booster seat before folding her own hands along with them as she led them in morning prayers. Our Father, Hail Mary, Glory Be, a Thank You for This Food prayer, and then they were allowed to eat.

Her heart pounded in her throat as she slid the bulky plastic climber to the rear corner of the living room. The she turned the television back on and popped the only secular video they owned into the VCR. Both girls stopped eating for a moment, their eyes bright with surprise as the first strains of the theme music from the movie *Babe* lilted through the apartment.

"Mama, why?" Anna asked, waffle and syrup peeking through her wide smile.

Krissy was cold with fear. This was it; the tape was in. The seal of normalcy had been broken. There was no going back now.

The tape was in.

The tape was in.

The tape was in.

Krissy couldn't bring herself to look Anna in the eye. She was in and out of the kitchen with white trash bags and into their bedroom in a flash. "Because it's a special day!" she tried to sing back to her daughter, worried that the child would somehow notice the stress and fear in her voice. She set out their clothes for the day, then started shoving everything else from their dresser into a white trash bag. The more she piled into the bag the quicker she seemed to be moving. Krissy could feel herself gaining momentum. One trash bag full and tied and on to emptying their closet. The volume on the video was low and she could hear Anna talking to Grace in the other room. Krissy suddenly stopped; what was Anna saying to her little sister? She crept to the door, breathless.

"It's a special day, Gracie! Mama says it's a special day!"

"Why pessel?" Grace garbled back, her mouth obviously jammed with food.

Krissy heard Anna sigh, and all at once she wanted to laugh. "Not pessel, Gracie!! *Special*!"

"Why sssss-pessel?" Grace asked.

"I dunno. Lemme go see …" Krissy heard Anna say, and she nearly jumped back into the hallway.

"No, no! You sit down and finish your breakfast!" Krissy said, waving Anna back toward her chair.

"Why to-day pessel, Mama?" Grace asked, jamming a piece of sausage into her wide-open mouth.

Krissy took a couple of steps forward and looked out the front window. Then she tiptoed across the room to check and make sure that that shadow of feet could not be seen in the space under the front door. She listened carefully; anyone standing in the hallway? When she was absolutely sure that she would not be overheard, Krissy took a deep breath and tried to smile. "Because today, we're going on an adventure!"

Chapter 4

Ad number 1415 was very direct, a 'this-is -who-I-am-and-what-I'm-about' type of thing. Krissy read it and re-read it, then read through all the rest of the ads that were listed under 'Men Seeking Women', then read Dorian's ad a third time. It was different than the rest in that he didn't list his age, height, weight or interests, and his only requirement for a woman seeking to contact him was that she be between the ages of nineteen and thirty-five and slender. Krissy liked that; he seemed to her, at least on paper, to be a person of some depth and character. No insinuation that any woman answering his ad would have to share any deep interest in his hobbies, look any particular way or be willing to engage in anything sketchy in the bedroom. He only said that he had a strong set of beliefs and wanted to meet someone who might potentially share them.

Her mother stood at the sink washing dishes; dozens of mismatched pieces that she'd collected over the years, along with a couple of commemorative ceramic beer steins that her hoarder-boyfriend had brought home as a peace offering, of sorts, after Lenore had caught him flirting it up with some chunky bleached blonde at the local bowling alley. She glanced at her daughter disapprovingly as Krissy punched in the ad number and waited, her stomach jumping with a mix of nerves and anticipation. This was what nice, normal grown-ups did in order to find dates, she told herself. This was how busy people with full-time jobs, who were not in school and didn't want to go to bars, found people of the opposite sex to spend time with. There was nothing abnormal or weird about answering a personal ad, she tried to reassure herself as a pre-recorded message clicked on.

The man said his name was Dorian. He said that he was in his late twenties and had a bachelor's degree. He said that he had a job that he loved, working with kids, and that he was only a thesis away from earning his master's degree. He said that his spare time was filled mostly with keeping fit (running, more specifically) and reading. He said that he was looking for someone to spend time with, to go the movies with, to have dinner with. To just relax and have fun with. No pressure. No games. Let's just get to know each other and see where it goes. And oh, by the way, he reassured the listener, the slender thing wasn't all that important either. He joked that as long as the person listening to the message wasn't the lady-wrestler type, he was willing to at least meet and get to know just about anyone who was sincere and honest about themselves and willing to give him a shot, too.

Krissy liked his voice. It was deep and strong and masculine, not like the soft-touch Boy Next Door she'd so recently left behind. Her own voice shook as she left a short reply message, and her mother's home phone as a contact number.

Dorian called her back the next afternoon. They talked for about a half an hour, Krissy taking the call upstairs on the extension in her mother's bedroom. She didn't want to have to try and have a pleasant conversation under the weight of Lenore's disapproving glare.

Dorian had a good sense of humor and was as much of a chatterbox as Krissy was, but within minutes Krissy found herself unable to squeeze a word in edgewise. Dorian had a lot to say and there were points in the conversation that Krissy didn't know if he was being sarcastic or serious, and he chuckled in a sort of condescending way when she asked. She was already wondering if she even wanted to bother meeting this overbearing know-it-all when he suddenly asked her where she might like to go on their date. Krissy was surprised and flattered; she'd thought at points in the conversation that Dorian was thinking that she was kind of slow on the uptake or maybe even a little dumb, but he was clearly interested in her and that made her want to give him a chance. She told him that she really wanted to go the county fair.

"Nooooo!" he replied, dragging the word out as though it were the stupidest idea he'd ever heard.

"No?" Krissy was taken aback. His reaction was so quick and overtly negative that for a moment she thought that he was joking.

"I'm not driving all that way and paying admission to smell cow shit and watch pig races! How about a movie and dinner? There's a new romantic comedy ... "

Krissy didn't know what to do. The only reason that she'd even looked at the ads was because she'd wanted a date to the fair. But this Dorian guy wasn't budging; going to the fair wasn't up for discussion, and he just kept talking. "What kind of food do you like? We'll go anywhere you want."

Krissy paused. It was a date, after all, and he was a grown up; no struggling college kid. He had a car and a job and he did seem genuinely interested in her. And it would just bug the hell out of Lenore if she went out with him. But he seemed so arrogant. So abrasive and pushy. " ... or we could skip the romantic comedies. What about an action flick? Or Gremlins Two! You wanna see a kid flick?" Dorian laughed; a genuine, lighthearted laugh that almost put Krissy at ease.

What was the harm, she wondered; it was just dinner and a movie. Saturday night at five-thirty was what they agreed on. Gremlins Two and dinner somewhere. Krissy had a knot in her stomach as she hung up the phone. She really didn't want to have to meet Dorian, let alone spend time with him, but even as she was bounding down the stairs and faking happy while she announced to her obviously annoyed mother that she'd made a date for that weekend, she knew that she was going to go out with him, anyway. It was a date and he was paying and maybe he would be different in person. Maybe it would be fun. If nothing else, it would be an evening away from her sullen mother and that house; that dirty, cluttered house that made Krissy feel as though she was being crushed from the inside out every time she walked through the front door.

Leaving Dorian

Linda Dynel

Chapter 5

"What's an adventure mean?" Anna asked. Luckily, her attention was divided between her breakfast and the television, so she wasn't really listening to Krissy's answer.

"Oh, you'll see!" Krissy tried to sound reassuring as she headed back to the girls' bedroom.

She whisked everything off of the rack in the closet and jammed the clothing, still on hangers, into a garbage bag. She looked at their toy box and their kitchen play set against the wall and all of their stuffed animals and hoped that at some point she would be able to collect all of that for them, too. Her brother had told her not to bother packing anything unnecessary, especially not toys; he was also getting divorced and his two young sons lived with him part time, so he had toys and games to spare. And besides, once her own divorce was final, she'd most likely get everything back that belonged to the girls, anyway. If not, he said, she could simply buy new.

Krissy dragged the two trash bags full of clothes out of the bedroom and into the kitchen. She leaned them against the wall under a picture of The Blessed Mother holding the Infant Jesus. Our Lady of the Streets; it was her favorite image of Mary. She thought about taking it off the wall and jamming it in with the girls' clothes, but then didn't.

Only what was necessary.

Anna and Grace looked at the bags, then back at the television. Krissy took another trash bag and jammed her own clothes into it. Socks, underwear and bras were dumped from their short drawers haphazardly before being covered with sweatshirts and long sleeve t-shirts. Jeans were ripped off of their hangers from the bar in the closet. Krissy opened the bottom doors of the old buffet table that she used as a dresser and looked at the pile of summer clothes stacked neatly inside. They were all cheap drug store t-shirts and thrift store shorts but were mostly like new because she rarely wore them, even on the warmest days; light fabric and shorts didn't hide bruising very well.

All at once a flutter of excitement and recognition rose in Krissy's belly; she wouldn't have any bruising that summer! That summer she would be able to be comfortable and look just like every other young mom walking with her children in the park or at the grocery store. That summer she was going to be able to wear t-shirts and shorts every day if she wanted to! Fueled by the possibility of happiness yet to come, Krissy grabbed the whole pile of summer clothes from top to bottom and pushed them on top of her jeans in the garbage bag. As she was tying the bag closed, she noticed blood rising from a scrape on the top of her hand. She figured that she'd probably scraped it going in and out of the old wooden buffet, but since it didn't hurt, she decided that it didn't matter; she merely wiped her hand on the back of jeans and kept moving. Time was of the essence.

She dragged the bag out to the kitchen and set it against the other two. Both girls were done eating and were sitting quietly in their chairs watching the movie. Such good girls, Krissy thought. Such good girls who deserved so much better than the way that they were being forced to live. She'd been repeating that phrase over and over to herself the entire week, every time she started feeling unsure about whether or not she should leave Dorian; every time she questioned whether or not taking the girls away from their father was the right thing to do.

Krissy plucked Grace from her booster while Anna inspected the trash bags. "Why are our clothes in here, Mama?" she asked, poking at the bags with one sticky finger.

"I'll tell you in a little while," Krissy tried to smile and carefully checked her tone of voice as she guided the girls toward the bathroom. "Right now, we need to wash hands and brush teeth and get dressed. Someone is coming to meet you girls today, and you want to look nice when he gets here, don't you?"

"Who it, Mama?" Grace asked. "Who come to see ... oh, Mama! Boo-Boo!" Grace grabbed Krissy's hand, running one tiny index finger over the bloodied scrape that Krissy had already forgotten was even there.

"Me fix you, Mama ..." Grace had a tight grip on Krissy's hand and was pulling her into the bathroom.

We don't have time for this, Krissy thought, trying to pull her hand away from Grace as gently as she could. Then Grace stopped and looked up at her with what seemed to Krissy to be relief and maybe even surprise in her bright hazel eyes, and asked, "No Daddy-Boo-Boo, Mama? No Daddy-Boo-Boo?"

Krissy wanted to die. To crumble into a pile of dust right there on the bathroom floor. What had she allowed her children to see, to live with and to think was normal? Instead, she shook her head no and let her daughter clean the scratch with a bit of damp toilet paper, before putting a Scooby Doo Band Aid over part of it.

"All betta, Mama!" Grace announced, planting a gentle kiss on Scooby's face. Krissy bit the inside of her lip to keep from crying and wrangled the girls out of their pajamas. Time was ticking away.

What if he comes home right now, Krissy was screaming on the inside, as she lathered Grace's hands and helped Anna squeeze toothpaste onto her small blue toothbrush. What if he loses this job just like he's lost every other job he's ever had? What if he slams through the front door right now, already pissed off and frustrated and ranting that the job loss was her fault, only to find his daughters talking about a visitor that they were about to meet and their clothes piled in trash bags on the kitchen floor?

Krissy dried Grace's hands and brushed her teeth and gave Anna a good once over before sending the girls into their room to get dressed. They could watch television as soon as they were dressed, she told them, but they had to stay sitting on the couch like good girls; no running around or Mama would turn the movie off and they'd have to do school after all.

Guaranteed compliance, Krissy knew.

She gathered all of their toiletries, toothbrushes and her own makeup while they dressed. Once they were back on the couch, hunkered down with their stuffed animals, Krissy slipped the small ring of short keys off the hook in the kitchen and quietly made her way into the back bedroom. Her hands were shaking so badly, she didn't know how she was going to get the tiny keys into their locks in order to open the drawers.

She took one of Dorian's large canvas duffel bags from the top shelf of the closet and laid it wide open on the floor. Then she took a deep breath to steady herself before unlocking the top drawer of the filing cabinet that he'd jammed into the back of their closet. Inside of that drawer, wrapped in old towels, was his End of The World Arsenal.

The New Millennium had been a huge deal for Dorian. He'd been convinced that the prophesies in The Book of Revelation were about to come to pass and that he and his little family were going to be some of the very few souls that would be spared Eternal Damnation and the wrath of God the Father. Because of this, he'd tried to prepare for the impending doom as best as he could. He was sure that any Roman Catholics that were left behind would surely be persecuted by any non-believers that survived, and he wanted to be ready. He'd had Krissy stockpiling water and canned food for almost a year. He'd had her buy black plastic trash bags and duct tape to cover the windows, and had bought weapons of all sorts in order to protect them from any outsiders who might want to do them harm.

Krissy remembered when Dorian had started bringing the weapons home. They were all wrapped in plain brown paper with no store logos. She knew that some of what Dorian had purchased was illegal in New York State. On more than one occasion, she'd expressed her concern over harboring, in their home and around the girls, what was essentially contraband. Dorian had brushed her off time and again, calling her stupid and worse. He'd rant that that he'd never comply with the rules and regulations of a police state -

should things come down to that - once the New Millennium was upon them.

The first things Krissy unwrapped were the SAP gloves. She laid them on the bottom of the duffel bag. Next, she carefully unwrapped the stun baton. It was still in its original box, but she didn't know whether or not it was charged so she was extra careful laying it on top of the gloves. She had no idea how the thing worked, but it was scary just to be touching the box that it was in. Krissy thought for a moment, then took the stun baton back out and re-wrapped it in towels before putting it in the bag. Better safe than sorry.

The day after Dorian had brought the stun baton home, he'd woken up in a bad mood and had been yelling at Krissy since before breakfast. He'd been so loud that the landlord had called and asked him to please keep it down, explaining that their upstairs neighbor had called her and complained. Dorian had punished Krissy after that call, pulling her hair and twisting her arm behind her back until she apologized for being such a stupid bitch and almost getting them kicked out of their home. Later that same day, Krissy was curled up in one corner of their old couch, watching the mid-day news and trying to stay out of Dorian's way, when he pulled the stun baton out of the file cabinet and sat down at the kitchen table with it. He was thrilled with the almost two-foot-long weapon, spinning it around his head and thrusting it out in front of him like a light saber.

"I could take down a rampaging bull with this thing!" Dorian chortled happily. "In fact, I could probably even kill somebody with it, if I held it on 'em long enough! My Lord in Heaven, this thing is amazing!"

Disgusted with his glee at the weapon that Krissy was sure he'd never have occasion to use, and doubly so since he'd come home with it the same day that he'd told her not to bother running to AmVets to scour the racks for used winter clothing for the girls because they had no extra money. She took one last shot at him, even though her shoulder and wrist were still smarting from his earlier attack against her.

"So, how long before you decide to zap me with that?" she snapped.

"Well," he said thoughtfully, running one hand up and down the length of the shiny black stick, "if you're a good girl, I guess you'll never have to find out."

Krissy shuddered at the memory.

Next into the bag was the sand filled Billy club and then the four gas masks, two adult-sized and two child-sized. None of the masks had any filters in the round front chambers, a fact that she'd hesitantly pointed out to Dorian when they'd arrived in the mail from somewhere in the Middle East. He'd sighed as he looked them over and Krissy could see his rising anger starting to tense his shoulder muscles. Suddenly realizing that he'd not really known what he was buying, and that the items he'd so carefully selected weren't going to be able to protect anyone from anything, let alone poison gas, Dorian had pushed the box of masks across the table at Krissy. He'd told her to put them by the filing cabinet; that she didn't know what the hell she was talking about and that he'd look them over more carefully later.

Finally, Krissy unwrapped the bottles of pepper spray. She double checked that the locks were firmly on the triggers before re-wrapping the shiny black and red canisters and putting them into the bag. She zipped the bag closed with plenty of room to spare and re-locked the drawer. Then she unlocked the bottom drawer. Inside was a small fireproof box. She took the box out and set it on the floor next to the duffel bag. Birth certificates and social security cards were in there, along with the Title to the car and other such necessary documents. She wiggled the key for the fireproof box off of the ring and jammed it into her front pocket, then closed the bottom drawer and re-locked it. She set the keyring on top of the file cabinet before bringing the duffel bag and the fireproof box into the kitchen and setting them next to the garbage bags full of clothes.

Rule breaker! She tried to kid with herself. You know the keys for the file cabinet are supposed to be hung RIGHT BACK WHERE YOU FOUND THEM!

Yes, they were. Unfortunately, there wasn't even cold comfort in leaving them out of place; in breaking that one small house rule. Not putting them back made Krissy feel uncomfortable, and she was about to go and get them when she realized that she hadn't even had a cup of coffee yet that morning. She was running water into the coffee pot, breathing deeply and trying to stop her hands from shaking, when she heard a gentle tapping on the front door.

Linda Dynel

Chapter 6

Dorian picked her up right on time that Saturday night. She felt funny riding in a stranger's car; though she'd known that he was a few years older than her, their age gap was even more pronounced once they met and were able to talk face to face. She was twenty-one going on thirteen; he was twenty-six going on fifty. But he was also friendly and funny and seemingly forthcoming about his crazy family and his screwed-up childhood. Krissy felt comfortable opening up to him about her own horrible childhood, as well as the struggles she was still trying to cope with at home. They watched the movie and ate dinner and had a drink and talked. When he dropped her back at her mother's house that night, they shared a very long goodnight kiss.

Two days later he called her early in the morning and offered to drive her to work so she wouldn't have to take the bus. On the way, he got stopped for driving through a stop sign. He laughed it off when the police officer walked away, apologizing that he was going to end up getting her to work late, though it was technically her fault; if she wasn't so damned beautiful, his eyes would have been on the road and not on her. Krissy blushed when he asked to see her again.

That Saturday night Dorian picked her up and took her back to his place. They sat on the floor of his tiny, stuffy efficiency apartment and talked. She cried about what a mess her life was and he wrapped his arms around her and pretty soon he was on top of her. He wanted to take her to bed. She said she wasn't sure. He said that he needed her. She said she liked him a lot, but that she wasn't sure if it was the right thing to do.

He said that he understood if she wasn't mature enough to enter into a more meaningful adult relationship; she did still live at home, after all. She hadn't finished college and didn't hold a great paying job. She was essentially still a kid, he lamented. Maybe their relationship should end right there. He offered to take her home, but since home was the one place that she was certain she didn't want to be, she said that she'd rather stay.

He undressed her in the darkness of his bedroom as they lay side by side on a mattress on the floor. She let him kiss her and touch her and though it scared her it also made her feel grown up and exhilarated. Then when he climbed on top of her and shoved one of her legs aside with his knee and she asked him whether or not he was going to wear a condom, he said he wouldn't finish inside of her. She thought about arguing but didn't.

She knew she could still get pregnant even if he didn't finish. She knew she could get any number of diseases if he didn't wear a condom. She wasn't even sure that she wanted him inside of her, but she didn't speak up; didn't say a word. She just lay there and let him penetrate her. Even though it hurt, she tried to pretend that it felt good, until she started to cry.

She wasn't sure where the tears were coming from; what their reason was. She was only sure that she was uncomfortable and that she wanted to leave. When Dorian realized that she was crying he stopped moving inside of her and asked her what was wrong, trying hard to sound caring though the edge in his voice spoke volumes of frustration and annoyance. She could only say that she didn't know. He pulled out until she stopped crying but then made one final push and finished inside of her anyway. Krissy gasped, horrified and in pain. When Dorian finally caught his breath and rolled off of her, he told her that she was just too damned hot and that he couldn't help himself. Then he lay next to her, his arm over Krissy's belly.

Linda Dynel

"Go to sleep, baby. You can clean up in the morning." With that, Dorian promptly fell asleep.

Krissy lay awake for hours while Dorian snored gently next to her. She wanted to get up and take a shower. She wanted to get dressed and go home, but she didn't move. She tried to relax and re-frame the evening in her mind. He really likes me, she told herself. He made a special effort to drive me to work; even got a ticket on the way! She told herself that he couldn't keep his hands off of her. That he thought she was pretty. Special. Hot.

Krissy shoved the feelings of guilt and shame and disgust with herself and with Dorian further and further down until she was able to relax and let her mind float away. She finally fell asleep just before sunrise.

Linda Dynel

Chapter 7

"Eggy here, Mama! Eggy here!"

Krissy could hear Grace's tiny feet land on the floor and pound toward the door. Grace loved Peggy Stubbs, their landlady. Peggy was a masculine woman whom Krissy guessed was in her mid-fifties, but who carried herself like a teenager. She was bold and happy and always had a smile for the girls. Since she was the only visitor they ever had, it was a real event for Anna and Grace when she came over, even if it was only for a few minutes, in order to collect the rent or to come in and fix something.

"No, I don't think its Miss Peggy ..." Krissy spoke softly as she tip-toed gingerly to the door, waving Grace back toward the couch. She held her breath as she put an eye to the peephole. Goosebumps covered her from head to toe when she saw her brother's ample lips and broad nose poking cartoon-like toward the looking glass.

For the first time all morning, Krissy was excited. It had been years since she'd had contact with Spence. Then one afternoon he'd come into Alfie Toaster's with his wife and their two sons. He hadn't known that she worked at the kid-friendly chain restaurant, and though it was awkward to try and reconnect in public and while she was at work, she could tell that it was glaringly apparent to Spence that something was terribly wrong in her life. It had been almost a decade since they'd seen each other face to face, Dorian had made sure of that, but her little brother could still read her like a book.

"If you ever need me, just call," Spence had told her, pressing his business card into her cold hand after his wife Chloe had taken their kids out to the car.

Krissy had hidden the business card in her wallet behind a picture of the girls. She wasn't sure why at the time; she knew that Dorian would never allow her to have any sort of real relationship with any of her family members ever again, and he'd certainly never allow his precious daughters to be anywhere near them. Still, Krissy had tucked the card safely away and prayed to God that Dorian wouldn't suddenly decide to go through her wallet and find it. A betrayal of that magnitude might, in Dorian's eyes, be too much to bear. Krissy didn't want to imagine what he'd do to her if he found the small white business card with her brother's handwriting scrawled across the back. And yet, she kept it. Curious, she'd thought more than once, that she would risk so much in order to keep a couple of phone numbers that she was sure she'd never have occasion to use.

Krissy opened the door slowly, trying to keep the tumblers on the deadbolt quiet. Spence was smiling, as was the young woman standing just behind him.

"Hey!" he breathed, wrapping his skinny arms around Krissy and hugging her so tightly she felt for a moment that she couldn't breathe.

"Hey!" she gasped.

When he finally let go, she could tell that he was just as scared as she was, though the young woman standing behind him was not. She looked curious, and happily defiant.

"Oh, Kris, this is Meagan."

"Hi!" The petite, curly haired girl reached out and shook Krissy's hand, but then must have thought better of it and gave Krissy a quick hug as well.

As Spence stepped into the apartment, his entire focus was on Anna and Grace. He had never met his nieces and was transfixed by the two little nymphs perched tidily on the edge of the worn, overstuffed sofa.

"Hi ..." he spoke to them with as much caution and self-control as he could muster. Krissy could tell that he was trying his best not to simply grab them up into his arms and smother them with hugs and kisses. Both girls merely sat there staring at him, wide-eyed and unsure.

"I'm your Uncle Spencer. I'm your mom's brother. It's nice to finally meet you two." He knelt down in front of them, his knees so close to their stockinged feet that Grace curled her toes back reflexively in order to avoid his touch.

"My mama's brother?" Anna asked, clearly surprised by this stranger's sudden claim on her family.

"Yep; I'm your mom's brother. That makes me your uncle. You're Anna, right?" Spence asked, trying his best to keep his distance, his balled-up fists set firmly on his thighs.

Anna nodded her head, smiling.

"Can I give you a hug, Anna?" Spence asked, holding out his arms to the hesitant child. Anna nodded her head again and Spence hugged her gently, though Krissy knew that if he had his way, her brother would have swept Anna up in his arms and hugged her until she giggled with delight. He had grown into such a fine man in the years that she'd been away.

Grace had curled herself up around the stuffed lamb she was holding and was seemingly trying to burrow into the back of the couch, so that when Spence finally released Anna, he knew not to offer a hug to the obviously frightened child. He simply held up his hand for a high five, though when she shook her head in refusal, Meagan stepped in and sat down next to Grace. She introduced herself and asked Grace what her little lamb's name was. Grace smiled and spoke quietly to Meagan, then uncurled herself a little and sat up in between Anna and Meagan after Spence stood up and tried to get his bearings.

It was the two-foot by three-foot print of Jesus that hung over the TV stand that initially caught Spence's attention, once he could focus on something other than his nieces. The picture was brooding and dark and it made Spence more and more uncomfortable the longer he looked at it. When he was finally able to shift his gaze, he realized that there was no end to the oddities that decorated the walls of his sister's sparsely furnished apartment. A large gold and silver crucifix hung just above a small shelf over the couch. On the shelf there was a tall, church type candle burning and a small glass bowl next to that filled with a little bit of cloudy water. There was also a small statuette of the child Jesus dressed in a colorful gown and crown and a couple of rosaries. There were ancient images of the Virgin Mary hung on either side of the shelf and on the walls of the dinette, as well.

Spence was about to comment on the large sign taped to the far wall of the dining room that read 'Our Lady of the Rosary School' as well as the colorful alphabet and numeral posterboards and all of the religious images hung underneath it, when a noise in the hallway drew his attention back to the living room and all of the weirdness therein. "What the f---" he started, then remembered that there were little people in the room. "What *is* all this??"

"This is the Divine Mercy image," Krissy explained, pointing to the picture over the TV stand. "It's Dorian's favorite. This is a Family Altar; there's Holy Water and the Infant of Prague and..." She was starting toward the kitchen but then stopped and looked back at her brother. He and Meagan were giving each other a look that said, "Crazy! Crazy!"

For just a moment Krissy felt offended. She and Spencer had not been raised with any sort of a faith life, and her conversion to Roman Catholicism had been a source of contention between her and her family in the few months after her Confirmation that she was still talking to them. But her faith was literally the only thing that was getting her through the horrific odyssey that leaving Dorian was turning out to be, and she didn't like to think that Spence might minimize or not understand that. But then Krissy tried to think how her tiny apartment must look to these two outsiders. It was mostly empty, save for some cheap furniture and the huge playground climber in the living room. A couple of pressed board bookshelves packed tightly with religious books and homeschool materials as well as a large variety of religious statuettes and framed religious images. Crucifixes and rosaries here and there. Dried palm leaves stacked atop her dining room curtains. Sheets of lined preschool writing paper with prayer reminders for her and the girls tacked to the dining room walls beside the homeschool posters. Yes, she reminded herself, this *was* "Crazy! Crazy!", and that's why she had to leave.

"Do you want to start getting the car packed?" Krissy asked as cheerfully as she could. She was going to let Spence's sideways glance at Meagan go, because the bottom line was that her brother didn't have to be there. He didn't have to help her. She said a short, silent prayer of thanksgiving that he was there at all.

When Spence saw what little Krissy had packed, he started looking around the apartment. "I know I said to only bring the bare necessities, but we've got two cars now, mine and Meagan's and ... we're still going to get yours, right?"

Krissy caught her breath. Yes, the next leg of their journey. After packing the cars and leaving her apartment behind, they were going to drive over to where Dorian worked and take their car. Or rather, *her* car. The car was in her name only, as Dorian had an atrocious driving record and plenty or outstanding parking tickets. When she'd told Spence days before that Dorian considered it *his* car, Spence had assured her that not only was it completely legal for her to take the car, it was also an imperative.

Krissy had been talking to Spence from work all week. She was stressed and distracted every moment that she was there, though she continually tried to keep the details of her disastrous personal life from as many of her co-workers as possible. No one at the restaurant had ever met Dorian; he'd never come into Alfie Toaster's in all the time that she'd worked there. But she was inordinately preoccupied with the fear that he would suddenly show up at the restaurant at some point that week and would somehow figure out what was going on; maybe see her talking on the phone through the restaurant's tall front windows and question her when she got home at night about who she'd been talking to and just what the hell was going on. She had no friends, only co-workers. She had no family, other than him and the girls. There was no good, reasonable explanation
why she would be talking to anyone on the phone.

But it was during one of her last conversations with Spence that Krissy decided that he was right; she had to take the car. "If you leave him with transportation, he'll have a way to get around. He'll spend all day and night trying to find you."

So, it was decided; she would have to have Spencer drive her to Dorian's work after they'd loaded up the car and the kids. She would have to walk into the parking lot and drive her car away, even though that meant risk being seen. Risk Dorian coming out and running after her. Risk everything, because she could not leave that one vital piece of their life behind. She had to hold all the cards, and their rusty old Celica was one of the most important.

"What else do you want to bring, Kris?" Spence asked after taking her few bags out to his car while Meagan sat on the couch with the girls and read to them from their Children's Bibles. "There's gotta be more." Spence looked around, but at that point even he looked skeptical.

Krissy thought about it. "Well, there's boxes of the girls' clothes in the basement. Anna's old things I've put away for Grace, and all of their summer clothes."

"Let's go!" Spence was out the front door in a flash, standing at the bottom of the steps in the hallway, hands on his hips. "We gotta get as much as we can right now and go, Kris. I don't want the girls in that looney bin for one more second. Let's drag whatever we can from the basement and just get the fuck outta here. Oh, yeah," Spence paused. "Meagan actually came along so that we wouldn't have to bring the girls with us to pick up your car. Just in case anything happens when we're getting it, ya' know? She's gonna take the girls in her car to the McDonald's on Niagara Street and wait for us there."

Just in case anything happens when we're picking up the car. Krissy swallowed hard. *The girls shouldn't be there, just in case anything happens.* She tried not to think about what that meant, the very real possibilities of what could happen if Dorian saw her there, getting out of Spencer's car and heading toward the Celica. She tried to push the images out of her mind and headed down into the basement with Spence.

The two dragged up three large boxes of the girls' clothes and shoved them into the trunk of Meagan's car, then grabbed the few stuffed animals and toys that Meagan had realized there would be room for and graciously helped the girls choose. Krissy told the girls to give her a hug and a kiss goodbye; that they were going for a ride in Meagan's car while she and Uncle Spence ran an errand.

Linda Dynel

Meagan walked the girls out of the apartment while Krissy ripped a sheet of paper from one of Dorian's notebooks and hurriedly scrawled him a short note. She left it on the kitchen counter under his favorite coffee mug. He was sure to see it. Then she grabbed her keys and her purse and double checked each room; had she forgotten anything? Left anything behind that she and the girls might need? Spence was at the front door, keeping watch.

"You ready?" he asked as Krissy grabbed her fleece jacket from the front closet, double checking in there as well. She grabbed two more of the girls' coats and an old pair of Anna's sneakers from the floor and then without saying a word, went back into the kitchen and grabbed a small sandwich bag full of candy and a couple of packets of fruit snacks from one of the cabinets. She jammed them into the pockets of her jacket as she motioned Spence out the front door.

Anna nearly jumped into the back of Meagan's car, while Grace cautiously followed behind her big sister. After many hugs and kisses and reassurances from Krissy, the girls were strapped into car seats and both Spence and Meagan were pulling out of the apartment building's parking lot in their separate directions: Meagan and the girls to the safety of a McDonald's parking lot on the other end of town, Spence and Krissy to the school where Dorian worked with at-risk youth.

Linda Dynel

Chapter 8

It was just past seven on Sunday morning when Krissy came creeping in, trying to make sure that a sleeping Lenore didn't wake up and realize that her daughter had not come home the night before. Krissy closed the heavy wooden front door behind her, then as she was turning to start up the stairs to her bedroom, she caught sight of one of Lenore's around the corner in the living room. Krissy took a step up onto the landing and could see that her mother was still dressed in pajamas and her heavy winter robe. One of her legs was bobbing furiously over the other, a sure sign that she was angry. Krissy took a deep breath, then turned on her heels and slowly made her way into the living room where her mother was seated tightly against one end of the sagging brown couch. She had a lit cigarette clutched tightly between her fingers.

"What the hell do you think you were doing last night?" Lenore asked tersely.

"What?" Krissy tried to sound as innocent and unaware as possible. You did not challenge Lenore. You did not defy Lenore. Lenore was always right and was to be complied with. Always. You didn't ever risk Lenore's wrath.

"You don't come home? I had no idea where you were, and you don't come home? How long have you known this guy? A week? And you don't even have the common courtesy to call?" Lenore was winding up, Krissy could tell. It might only be a matter of moments before she was up and off the couch and screaming in her daughter's face.

Krissy tried to sound penitent, though it was a tough sell. All she could think was: this from a woman who left her children for a solid year in order to shack up with her hoarder-boyfriend? This from a woman who had, in the past, come home so black and blue with hickeys that it looked as though someone had tried to strangle her the night before? But Krissy didn't say any of that out loud, nor did she let the utter contempt and loathing she felt for her mother show on her face. Instead, she reached deep down inside of herself and tried to cry. It made Krissy sick to her stomach to have to do it, but it also made her sick to her stomach to have to live in that house with the woman who'd given birth to her but was of no more use to her in any real way than anyone else in her family. Grandparents who had moved away in their retirement and left her with this crazy lady as her only source of support and guidance. Aunts and uncles who had given up and stopped checking in on her and Spence the deeper Lenore had fallen into mental illness and her own self-pity, both of which she fueled with a steady stream of alcohol, prescription medication and indecent men.

Krissy's heart was racing. She just needed her mother to back off for a few seconds, just enough time for her to retreat up to the safety of her bedroom. Working the lump of anxiety that was slowly closing her throat, she tried to make the tears that were finally starting to surface from the night before work to her advantage. "I'm sorry, Mom; I just didn't think. I..."

"You are goddamned right you didn't think! What the hell is the matter with you, Kris? You have one date with this guy and the next thing you know, you're in his bed? What the hell is that? Is that how you were raised, to act like some kind of whore?"

Well, as a matter of fact, Krissy thought, but knew not to say a word. Instead, she hid her face in her hands in feigned shame and bolted out of the room and up the stairs. She locked the bedroom door behind her once she was safely inside. Hypocrite, she screamed at her mother in her head, tears streaming down her face as she sat cross legged on the thin, vinyl covered mattress that lay kitty corner on the floor between the piles of junk and cardboard boxes.

Mickey curled into Krissy's lap and she hugged the scrawny little cat and cried, letting her warm tears run dark black stripes down his coarse, short coat. Dorian had been right the night before, she thought, when he'd said that while every family was a little screwed up, that his family, and hers as she'd described them, seemed a little more screwed up than most. He'd said that he felt sorry for her having to be raised by a woman who was so obviously imbalanced, but who also seemed just downright mean. He also knew how much it sucked to have your dad living out of the house because of a divorce, though he thought that Krissy's situation growing up had been far sadder and more unsettling than his had ever been. At least his dad was still in the picture on an almost weekly basis.

Being raised without a dad, with no man to protect and look after her? Dorian said that he thought that that was just about the worst personal loss that any little girl could suffer. He praised Krissy for handling it so well and for surviving a childhood that had been wrought with so much neglect and emotional abuse. And, he'd whispered in hushed tones as they sat across from each other on his living room floor, it was amazing that she'd survived the sexual abuse. Krissy had been dumbfounded and astonished that he'd been able to figure that out about her; the fact that she'd suffered more than one trauma of that sort as a little girl. He'd said that he could tell just by the way she carried herself that she was a young lady who felt that she needed to protect herself, and he respected that. But he assured her that she would never have to protect herself from him. He was different. He respected her, and he would never think of hurting her. But then he'd taken her to bed and he had hurt her, hadn't he?

Krissy dried her tears and tried to ignore the ache that was twisting her stomach into knots. Dorian was a guy like every other guy, she told herself. He wanted sex, but that didn't mean that everything he'd said to her was a bunch of bull crap. He was smart and intuitive and understanding. It had been nice to be able to open up to someone about her family and not have to be careful of what she said for fear that she would be looked at as a loser, or worse, because of the actions of the people she happened to be biologically connected to. Dorian really seemed to understand her, and he really seemed to like her. In fact, he seemed almost smitten with her. The night before hadn't been all bad, she lied to herself, trying to re-write the anxieties and shame that kept trying to creep back into her heart. He was just a guy doing what guys did.

Once Krissy heard Lenore's bedroom door slam, she knew to wait fifteen minutes or so before opening her own. She decided that as soon as the coast was clear she would make her way downstairs and try to find something to eat while she went through the paper and looked at ads for apartments. Every part of Krissy, every tiny shred of her body, mind and soul, screamed for her to get the hell out of her mother's house. The morning's paper would surely still be in the dining room, on top of one of the stacks of old daily and Sunday newspapers that Lenore allowed her hoarder boyfriend to keep all over the desperately filthy house.

Chapter 9

Krissy waved to Anna and Grace as Meagan's car pulled past Spence's. Anna looked happy and excited; Grace fearful and apprehensive. Those were her girls, those two tiny faces getting smaller and smaller as they were driven away in a near stranger's car. She had never left the girls alone with anyone before. Not a babysitter. Not any of Dorian's family members. No one. Babysitters could easily be molesters, Dorian had cautioned. His family was crazy and shouldn't be trusted, unless he was right there to monitor their every word and interaction. Be a mother, he'd growled at Krissy the one time she'd wondered out loud if she shouldn't enroll the girls in some organized play group, maybe at the YMCA. Some place she could stay and watch while they played with kids their own age, just so that they weren't cooped up in the house all day long with only each other for company.

"What the hell are you talking about?" Dorian had asked her suspiciously, puffing up his chest and sliding one finger over his unshaven upper lip. He'd looked at her like he was trying to figure something out. Then his eyebrows raised. "I know! You're trying to get out of having to homeschool the kids! You horrible, wretch of a mother! And what are *you* gonna be doing while the girls are playing with all those filthy, secular toys that all those unkempt, snot nose kids have also been playing with, huh? You gonna talk to the other mommies? You gonna make friends? You gonna maybe flirt a little with the single dads that are there; assholes trolling for some bored, stupid stay-at-home mom who's just lookin' for a little attention? You're willing to risk the health and well-being and mental stability of my daughters so you can go and gossip with a bunch of filthy whores and maybe get groped by some homeboy who decided that playgroup is the new hot spot to find an easy piece of ass?! Oh, that's rich!"

But they weren't cooped up in the house, now, were they? Nope. Now they were waving goodbye to her, being driven away by a woman named Meagan that Krissy had met only minutes before but who now quite literally had the lives of her precious daughters in her hands. Dorian would have gone ballistic if he'd pulled up just then. Crazier, Krissy was sure, than she'd ever seen him before. She took a deep breath and tried to calm down; tried to push the image out of her mind.

Spence looked both ways as they pulled out of the parking lot and onto Gray Street, then looked again. It seemed to Krissy that he was looking for more than just traffic; his fingers were tapping the steering wheel and his cheeks were flushed.

"What the fuck was all that, Kris; all those pictures and rosaries and bullshit everywhere? And that huge picture of Christ with the candles? What the hell was that?" His voice was shaky and he was almost shouting, though Krissy knew he didn't realize it.

"Are you O.K?" she asked hesitantly.

He looked at her like she had a screw loose, but finally sat back into his seat. "Yeah, Kris, I'm fine. But I'm worried about you... and the girls. Jesus Christ, Kris... how did you live like that every day? How did you..."

"Take a right here," she interrupted him, pointing to an upcoming cross street.

They were both silent for a minute, Krissy glancing at Alfie Toaster's as they drove past it. She wouldn't be working at that location for a while. Her store manager, Dan, had worked out a plan almost overnight with their district manager so that Krissy could still work while she and the girls were in hiding. She would work at the Alfie Toaster's near Spence's house under an assumed name. She would only waitress, not work in management like she did at her own location. Both men knew that it would mean she'd lose at least half of her set pay, but everyone agreed that half pay was better than no pay, and Krissy was just grateful that the manager at the Hamburg unit was willing to work with her at all. He'd been told the entire truth about what she was going through and understood that if Dorian found out where she was working, that he could be setting himself and his entire staff up for trouble. But the man hadn't flinched. He'd told both Dan and her district manager to have Krissy stop by and see him once she was settled in at her brother's. He would work things out for her, no problem.

"Kris, that... that crap... that's not normal. You know that, right? I mean..."

"Well, we are Roman Catholic!" Krissy's answer was sharper than she'd intended it to be and she immediately wished she'd said nothing.

Spence looked wounded. His voice softened and he took a deep breath before he spoke again. He knew that there was a lot of work that he and everyone else who loved Krissy was going to have to do; careful, meticulous work to keep Krissy from getting scared and overwhelmed and feeling as though her best option was to simply go back to Dorian.

"I know, Kris. I didn't mean to... I wasn't trying to make fun of that stuff. It's just that... do you think most Catholic families have that stuff in their houses? All the pictures and little statues and weird shit all over the place? I mean, I've known Catholic families before, Kris, and I don't remember there ever being shit like that... to that extreme... hell... maybe a cross or some dried palm leaves... maybe a picture of The Last Supper... I know it's meant to be religious, but Jesus, Kris... it just comes off so friggin' creepy."

Krissy bristled, but tried not to let it show. She bit her tongue and swallowed hard.

"Don't be mad, Kris. I was only trying to say that..."

"I know, Spence," she decided to say the words that he needed to hear. She would say them because intellectually she knew that they were true, even if in her heart she was still struggling to get on board in believing them fully herself. "I know that none of that is normal. It's not true Roman Catholicism; it's Dorian's version."

Dorian's voice was ever present in her head, running on a constant loop. She hoped to silence that voice, but was scared of what she would hear in its place. If not Dorian's directives, then whose? If he wasn't keeping her and the girls on the right path, what path were they going to take? There were moments in the past week that Krissy had felt as though she had the world by the horns and that she was absolutely sure that she was going to be completely fine without him, in more ways than she could imagine. Then there were moments that she wasn't sure how she was going to raise the girls over a full twenty-four-hour period without the structure and directives that Dorian had always provided.

"Thank you!" Spence pounded the steering wheel with both hands so forcefully that it made Krissy jump. "Oh, sorry!" he almost laughed. "But Jesus Christ, Kris... God... I guess I just needed to hear you say that, ya' know? Fuck! Thank God, Kris! Wow... you know... I really do think you're gonna be O.K!"

The constant taking of the Lord's name in vain was beginning to wear on Krissy a little, but she breathed and reminded herself that Spence was risking his own safety and wellbeing in order to help her and the girls. He didn't have to do it and neither did Meagan, and that as adults they had every right to speak any way they chose. She just hoped that he'd ease up with the swearing once they were all back at his apartment and the girls were within earshot.

"Here; turn left here," Krissy pointed to a tree lined side-street. The school where Dorian worked was only a couple of blocks farther. As Spence slowly pulled down the narrow residential street, Krissy started to feel warm and sick and overwhelmed.

"Where's the staff parking lot?" he asked as he stopped just next to the school.

"Just around back, to the right." Krissy scooted down in the seat. She wanted to shrink, to become a speck; a tiny gnat that Dorian would not be able to see if for some reason he happened to be looking out the window at just the wrong moment.

As Spence drove slowly past the building, Krissy said a silent prayer of thanksgiving that it had been raining on and off all morning. Dorian would definitely be inside; there would be no taking the kids out on the playground or to the basketball courts.

A wave of nausea rose in her throat as Spence pulled into the staff parking lot. Every muscle was tight and she could feel herself sweating. She wanted to cry. She wanted to run. Istead, she said, "Stop! It's right there; that white one!"

Spence looked at her quizzically. "That? Is it even going to start?"

Krissy took a deep breath. She hadn't thought about the car not starting. She swallowed the lump that was still rising in her throat. "I hope so. It started this morning."

She fished her keys from the front pocket of her jacket; the jacket that she'd gotten free by collecting UPC codes. Dorian was never happy when she spent money on herself, so when the offer for the plush fleece zip-up had appeared in the Sunday supplement, Krissy had immediately started saving the macaroni and cheese UPC's in order to get it. The jacket fit her perfectly and she loved its deep green color. It was one of the small joys in her life.

Spence grabbed her arm as she went to get out. "You get in and drive like a bat out of hell; I'll be right behind you."

This was it; this was the final step. She was going to take the car. She was going to take the car and drive away.

Away.

Away, away, away.

Her hand was cold and clammy as she opened the door. She slammed it shut harder than she meant to and bolted the six or seven steps between Spencer's car and her own. Dorian always locked the doors, but he also used a safety bar on the steering wheel so that the car couldn't be stolen. It was the one thing that Krissy still made fun of him about, especially when she knew she was going to get a beating anyway and decided to get a lick of her own in just because. Who in the world would want to steal their crappy car, she'd needle him, squinting her eyes defiantly. The beating would be no worse for her commentary and it still felt good to fight back once in a while, if only a little.

She had the door unlocked and the safety bar off in seconds. She put the key in the ignition and even as she was starting a Hail Mary, the engine turned over. She wanted to throw up. Instead, she started to cry. Huge, fat tears streamed down her cheeks as she pulled in front of Spence's car and sped out of the parking lot. He

Leaving Dorian

was right behind her; she could see him following close in the rearview. She knew where she was headed. The McDonald's on Niagara Street; Meagan would be waiting for them there. They'd stop just long enough for Krissy to put the girls into her car, then she would follow both cars to Spence's house in the South towns.

She looked in her side mirror. She looked in her rearview. She craned her neck to look behind her car and Spence's car at the first stop sign.

No Dorian.

No Dorian?

She'd been terrified. She'd thought that he would know, that he would be able to maybe sense, or feel, or maybe ... She felt uncomfortable even admitting it to herself, but she'd wondered if maybe he wouldn't have had some strange, spiritual way of knowing that she was there. That somehow he'd know what it was that she was doing.

And yet, there was no sign of Dorian.

She breathed a sigh of relief and realized that she wasn't crying anymore.

And she was out.

Out?

Yes.

She was out.

Chapter 10

Krissy hadn't been staying with her mother for more than a few weeks when Lenore made it clear that it was time for her daughter to go. Krissy had been coming downstairs late one Saturday morning wearing only the flimsy nylon nightgown and cotton panties that she'd worn to bed, and hadn't realized that Lenore's boyfriend was even in the house. Since he was on his way out the front door, by the time she reached the bottom of the stairs he was standing right there in front of her. Krissy was surprised to see him, to be sure, but he made some silly comment about her sleeping all day and she joked back and when he put his arms out to hug her good bye she let him.

It wasn't until later that day that Krissy realized that her mother was angry. Lenore wasn't one to talk things out; sometimes when she was mad at you, she simply stopped talking to you. It was the flip side of her raging; her face turned to a mask of stone and you simply ceased to exist. It wasn't until Krissy was coming up from the basement with a basket full of laundry, hours after dinner, that Lenore broke her icy silence. She slammed a folded newspaper on top of the full laundry basket, almost knocking it out of Krissy's hands. Curling her lips back over her teeth, Lenore chortled that it was about time that Krissy spread her wings again and fly, fly away. Then she tapped the thin paper with one long, perfectly manicured fingernail and explained that she'd gotten Krissy started by circling a couple of nice-looking apartments in the city.

Then she growled, but with as much self-control as Krissy had seen her exercise in a very long time, that she would appreciate it if Krissy could manage to exhibit just a bit more modesty for the remainder of the time that she lived there. That walking around half naked made her look like a slut. And although she'd certainly acted like a slut by staying over at Dorian's that one Saturday night a couple of weeks before, that if she continued to advertise her newly found sexual freedom, at some point she was going to give some man the wrong impression and was going to get herself into trouble. Then she smiled sweetly and offered to go with Krissy to look at the apartments that she'd circled. She even offered to help Krissy out by buying whatever household goods she might need but couldn't afford; sheets, pots and pans, whatever. Because that's what mothers were for, after all; standing by their kids.

Krissy was stunned but tried not to show it. It wasn't the first time her mother had chosen a man over her children, and certainly not the first time that she'd become almost vicious in regards to Krissy's sexuality versus her own.

When Krissy was twelve, Lenore was dating an older man who had a slew of ill-behaved children, all in their teens and early twenties. Lenore would take Krissy and Spence over to his house at least a couple of nights a week and tell the pair to go and play with the boyfriend's kids. Smoking and drinking and getting high behind the old barn that sat back on the boyfriend's property were only a few of the oddities that Krissy and Spence were exposed to, along with plenty of seventies rock music played way too loudly and teenagers experimenting with their own burgeoning sexuality right in front of them.

But the biggest problem for Krissy was the man's middle child, Marcus. He was a husky seventeen-year-old who'd been allowed too many late nights with his older brothers and their friends and girlfriends while his dad partied with a variety of women, Krissy's mother included. He was always trying to touch Krissy's stomach and wanting to rub her back, and every once in a while, he would try and get her to sit on his lap. Spence was too young to know what was going on and all her mom would say when Krissy went hunting around the man's expansive farm house in order to find her and tell her that she was tired and ready to go home was that she needed to let Lenore have her time and to go and play with the other kids.

Then one night Marcus wouldn't take his hand off of Krissy's knee. They were driving in Lenore's car, Marcus sitting in the front in between Lenore and Krissy while Spence sat in the back. Lenore had taken a liking to Marcus in the months since she'd started dating his dad and Marcus was over at their apartment a lot. More than he should have been, Krissy thought. Lenore would only say that Marcus was a handful and a half and a burden to his father and that she was trying to take a little pressure off of his dad; teach him some responsibility, as she frequently had him help her cook and clean.

Marcus inched closer to Krissy and put his hand on her knee. When Krissy asked him to move it, he simply smiled at her and said no. Then Krissy reached over and took his hand and moved it off of her leg. He put it back on her knee with a grin. Krissy looked over at Lenore, who though she was driving had clearly seen the interaction but was choosing to pretend that she hadn't. Krissy ended up sitting there the rest of the ride with Marcus' hand on her knee, her skin crawling and desperately wanting to cry because she knew that her mother wasn't going to do anything about it. Marcus must have known, too, since he continued to smile and knead Krissy's knee with his chunky, sweaty fingers.

It was only a couple of weeks after the car incident that Krissy decided she'd had enough. Marcus had cornered her in the living room of her mother's apartment late one afternoon when he was supposed to be babysitting Krissy and Spence, refusing to let her move until she gave him a kiss on the lips. She'd said no and made a fuss and cried loudly enough to bring Spence out of his room to find out what was going on. Marcus had turned around just long enough for her to get away, where she locked herself in her room for the rest of the evening until her mother got home from work. She went to Lenore later that night and told her that Marcus was bothering her again, that he liked her but that she didn't like him back and that she wanted Lenore to make him stop touching her.

Instead of asking her daughter what had happened that afternoon, Lenore flew into a rage.

"He doesn't *like* you! He's in love with *me*! He's always here whenever I need him, watching you two kids and helping me with chores! He's mine! Do you understand? *Mine*! He doesn't want you! You're just a little girl! What in the hell could he want with you? Don't give yourself so much credit, Kris! He's mine, and you need to stay the hell away from him, do you understand?"

Krissy felt as though she'd been slapped. She slunk off to her room and cried into her pillow until she couldn't cry anymore. She didn't understand. Marcus was just a kid; why would Lenore act that way about Marcus, like she was talking about her grown-up boyfriend? And why was she yelling at Krissy when all she had done was to ask for help? Krissy was scared and confused and dreading the next time that Marcus came over. Was Lenore going to have a talk with him and make him leave her alone? The fear and dread that swam in Krissy's belly over the next few days was almost as bad as the icy silent treatment that Lenore cast upon her daughter. But then she heard Lenore crying on the phone to Grandma Patty that it was over between her and the boyfriend and that she was thinking of moving herself and Krissy and Spence out of state for a fresh start. Krissy didn't know what had happened but was glad after a few weeks had gone by and she hadn't seen Marcus or his dad and realized that the boxes stacked in the corner of their kitchenette were packing boxes. The three of them were, indeed, moving.

They lived with family in Kentucky for almost two months before Lenore grew tired of job hunting and the family members grew tired of supporting her and babysitting Krissy and Spence. Having overstayed their welcome, Lenore and Krissy and Spence were packed up and back in Buffalo before the summer was over. Back to another crappy, run-down apartment. Back to Lenore's drunken stupors and manic fits and oddball boyfriends. Back to her sleeping her days away to escape a life she hated when nothing else would soothe her. But at least Marcus was gone for good; Krissy had been truly thankful for that.

Lenore kept her word and did take her daughter apartment hunting, though Krissy knew it was only to expedite the process of her moving out. Within two weeks Krissy had rented a small, third floor walk-up. Though it was basically two rooms and a closet, the landlord agreed to accept Mickey without any additional security deposits and Krissy was on her own again by the end of the month.

About a week after Krissy had moved, Lenore made a special point to visit. This time Lenore kissed her daughter goodbye and even offered to let Krissy cook her dinner sometime. Krissy didn't think her mother lit a cigarette after that goodbye until her feet were firmly planted on the sidewalk outside. Once Lenore was gone, Krissy looked around her drab, empty apartment and realized that she was basically all alone in the world. Mickey rubbed around her legs and she tried not to cry.

Then the phone rang. It was Dorian.

Linda Dynel

Chapter 11

Krissy pulled into the McDonald's parking lot and drove toward Meagan's car, which was parked near the back. Meagan was turned fully around in the driver's seat, laughing with the girls. When she noticed Krissy pulling in with Spence behind her, she bolted from her vehicle, slamming the door behind her. Krissy could see Anna and Grace looking to see where their new friend was going. Krissy pulled in right next to Meagan's car, but left the Celica running as she got out; sometimes when she turned it off it didn't want to start again right away and she didn't want to risk getting stuck.

"You did it!" Meagan sang, throwing her arms around Krissy's neck. "Oh, my God, you did it!"

Krissy was trying to be patient but she didn't feel much like celebrating just yet. She wanted to get the kids into her car and go. She could already see Anna trying to wriggle free from the booster seat she was still firmly strapped into. "Let's get the kids into my car and go; I just want to go."

She felt sick to her stomach. She was worried that Dorian would have somehow figured out that the car was gone; that maybe a co-worker would have seen his car driving away and gone in and told him that someone was stealing it. Krissy searched the street for any sign of him. Any sign of a police car, maybe, coming to look for the car. But all was quiet save for a very young lady pushing a stroller and a roofing crew installing a batch of new shingles on a little house just across the street.

Meagan leaned into the back seat and unstrapped the girls. They were covered in mess, all sticky hands and faces. Krissy kissed them both and asked how their second breakfast was. Anna was all full of commentary and stories but Grace just clung to Krissy's leg as she led them from Meagan's car to her own.

Anna immediately protested when Krissy directed her into her booster seat. "But Mama," she whined, holding up her hands as evidence that she could not. "Daddy says no riding in his car with messy hands!" Grace still clung to Krissy's leg, watching and waiting.

It was her car, Krissy reminded herself, no matter what Dorian said. The car was registered in her name and she worked and paid for gas and repairs just like he did. If she wanted to allow the girls to ride in the car with sticky hands and faces, that was up to her.

And yet, she paused.

Dorian said everything they owned was his and not hers. He was the man and she was the woman. How could she *own* property when she *was* property, he'd ask her over and over again. She was no different to him than the car, than the climber in the living room, than the toothbrush that he cleaned his teeth with. She was simply a thing. He was a man, perfect in the eyes of God, and she was his property, which gave her entrance into The Kingdom. Her only value lay in the fact that she was a part of him. Made from his rib. Flesh of his flesh, which was why he could do anything he liked to her. If he wanted to chop off one of her fingers, for instance, no one could stop him or tell him not to. That was his right. So, whatever he did to her to keep her holy and in line with Catholic teaching and free from sin was his God given right. Whatever rules he made, no matter how small, were to be followed simply because he had made them.

That's what Dorian said, but Dorian wasn't there.

It was her car, and they were her daughters, too.

"But Mama says you can ride in her car with messy hands, and with messy faces! So come on, now, let's get in," she took Anna by the arm and gently tried to move her into the back seat, but the child would not budge.

"But this isn't your car. It's Daddy's car, and Daddy says no riding in his car with messy hands."

Anna wasn't being disrespectful, just firm, because Anna was Daddy's Girl. Trying to figure out how she was going to raise Anna on her own was almost as scary a proposition to Krissy as leaving Dorian was.

Time to pull out the big guns, Krissy thought. She reached into the pocket of her jacket and pulled out a small, square caramel wrapped in clear cellophane. "This is Mama's car now, and Mama says you can ride in it no matter how messy you are. In fact, you can even eat in Mama's car! What do you think about that?"

Anna's eyes grew as big as saucers as she tried to process what it was that her mama was telling her. The information was confusing and she was trying hard to hold firm to her Daddy Rules, but that caramel was right there, just inches from her round face.

"I brought the whole bag, Anna Banana; they're all right here in my pocket," Krissy leaned over and opened her jacket's slash pocket just a bit so Anna could see the bag of candies inside. "You can have them all, right now! But I need you to get into your car seat or I can't give them to you." Krissy screwed up her lips to mirror the pensive face of her older daughter. She was prepared for anything; arguing, yelling, threatening - all things she'd never needed to do with her children in the past but was prepared to have to do at that very moment in order to save her own life.

And then all at once, blessed compliance.

"O.K, Mama." Anna climbed into the backseat and Grace let go of Krissy's leg and climbed in after her. Krissy strapped them both in, then handed a caramel to Anna and a packet of fruit snacks to Grace before closing the door and breathing a deep sigh of relief. Spence and Meagan gave her quick hugs and Krissy looked up and down Niagara Street one last time before getting into her car and fastening her own seatbelt.

No Dorian.

Not yet, anyway.

"You ready?" Spence yelled from his open car window.

Krissy nodded her head. She was ready.

Linda Dynel

Chapter 12

It only took one week of sleeping in her new apartment for Krissy to realize that she didn't like it there. She didn't feel safe. Her front door didn't seem to sit properly in its frame and she noticed that the dead bolt didn't always want to latch, especially on very humid days. Her bedroom was nothing more than a long, narrow closet, drywalled off from the apartment next door. Even that drywall hadn't been installed correctly, as evidenced by the fact that she could see right into her neighbor's apartment from a narrow crack that had been left between the exterior wall and the bedroom wall. On the far end of her bedroom there was another heavy door, much like her front door. It was dead bolted shut and there was old newspaper crumbled and jammed in between the space between the door and the frame so that anyone out in the hallway couldn't see into her bedroom. Laying there in bed, hot and uncomfortable because the one window in the room didn't allow for much air flow from the outside, Krissy tried not to listen to the guy that lived next door going at it with his girlfriend. She laid with a pillow over her head and tried to figure out what she was going to do about Dorian.

She didn't want to see him anymore.

That first night in her new place he'd brought over an extravagant dinner after he'd gone home to shower. They'd both had a long day moving her in, even though a bunch of her old college friends had helped them. She didn't yet have a couch or a decent TV, so the two sat at her old Formica kitchen table and she tried to stay awake while he poured her more wine than she wanted to drink. He made a flourish of taking her to bed, but she fell asleep as he was trying to undress her. He woke up angry and disgusted the next morning and made sure that she knew that she had disappointed him and ruined his evening. Before he left, he told her that he wasn't staying in that filthy little hovel of hers ever again. Why would she treat him like that, he wondered as he was putting on his shoes; invite him over just to shoot him down and make him feel like shit. Was she trying to make him feel like less than a man; was that her game? Now that she was an independent woman, on her own and away from her family, she was going to start acting all hardcore bitch? Treat him like a plaything? Like a money grab? Fuck you, he'd growled at her before slamming out the front door.

Krissy had sat at her kitchen table in the t-shirt and panties that Dorian had unsuccessfully tried to peel off of her the night before, reeling. What was he talking about, she wondered; he'd commented at dinner the night before that she'd seemed exhausted. He'd even caught her eyes closing after the second glass of wine he'd poured her and laughed a little, saying that she was a tired baby and needed to be put to bed immediately. And he'd done nothing but talk the place up the couple of times he'd seen it when she'd gone to clean before she'd moved in. Now he hated it there? Now he thought she was some horrible person who was using him, trying to get things from him and make him feel bad? There was something about Dorian that made Krissy's stomach hurt a little; something about him that made her feel a little bit uncomfortable and afraid.

The next day she called her best girlfriend Marnie and asked her to come over. She needed to talk. She told Marnie that she didn't want to see Dorian anymore; that she felt funny when she was with him and a little afraid and that he was so weird sometimes. He would be all loving and happy and fine, but then she could say or do the smallest thing and he would turn. Change. Get really angry or mean and sarcastic.

Marnie had helped her move in and had also met Dorian a couple of times before that, but she didn't like him and had made no bones about it. "He's an asshole, and he treats you like shit; how many times do I have to tell you that? Just break up with him!" she'd said without hesitation while chasing after one of her year-old twin sons that she'd brought with her to visit.

Krissy loved the twins and wished that she were a young mom like Marnie. Though Marnie was overwhelmed and in an unhappy marriage herself, she still seemed way more grown-up and mature than Krissy felt on her best days. Marnie had a family and a life of her own. All Krissy had was empty space and time to fill; a dead-end job that she hated and no money to go anywhere or to do anything fun. Even college seemed beyond her reach, unclear as she was about how she'd pay for it even if she did decide on a major.

"But I don't know if I can."

Marnie took a drag off of her cigarette and looked at Krissy in disbelief. "Whaddaya mean you don't know if you can? You're not married to the guy! Just break up with him!"

Krissy didn't know what she meant, either. Why couldn't she break up with him? Why would she even say that? She decided then and there that the next time Dorian called, she would simply tell him that she didn't want to see him anymore; nothing personal, just moving on. Sayonara Sunshine. There were plenty of other fish in the sea. Marnie agreed.

But the next day when Dorian called to make plans with Krissy and she hesitated, he asked her what was up. How had her visit with her friend Marnie gone? She told him fine, but wondered how he'd known that she'd seen Marnie. He said he'd driven by on his way to the grocery store and had noticed Marnie's car parked outside Krissy's building. He questioned her again, wondering if Marnie had said anything about him. Krissy lied and said no but then Dorian got angry and made snide comments about her trashy friend who had a husband and two kids but who still chose to wear a skimpy outfit to help Krissy move.

Why, Dorian asked Krissy, would her best girlfriend wear short shorts and a tank top to do manual labor? To impress her? Clearly not, unless she was actually a dyke. It had obviously been to impress him. Hadn't Krissy even noticed that? He speculated that Marnie had talked him down really good to Krissy the day before when she'd come over to Krissy's little hole in the wall apartment. He said that maybe the real reason Marnie was talking all kinds of shit about him was so that he and Krissy would break up and she would have the opportunity to make a move on him. Had Krissy thought of that, he asked through what sounded like clenched teeth. Had Krissy even considered the fact that her best girlfriend might be trying to wedge herself in between Krissy and Dorian for her own selfish gain?

Before Dorian hung up on her, he asked Krissy what kind of a person allows someone like Marnie to remain in her life; what kind of a girl allows herself to be controlled by a friend like that? A dumb girl, he barked at her, a dumb girl who doesn't give a shit about a guy who really cares about her and who was doing everything in his power to get her on her feet after her crazy-ass mother had basically kicked her out.

An hour later he called Krissy back and apologized for yelling at her. He told her he was only trying to protect her feelings. That he'd noticed Marnie checking him out all afternoon the day of the move and claimed that at one point he'd even stood with her at the truck in the driveway while Krissy was upstairs unpacking and told her to back up off of him, that he was Krissy's boyfriend and that she was making him uncomfortable. He claimed that Marnie said she didn't know what he was talking about but that she'd stopped staring at him and giggling and bending over in front of him after that. Dorian told Krissy that he cared about her and that he only wanted the best for her, but that sometimes it seemed like he wanted better for her than she wanted for herself. Then he asked her if she still wanted to make plans for that evening; he had a special Japanese restaurant in mind that he wanted to take her to.

Krissy heard the guy next door clomping up the rickety wooden steps and past her front door to his own, a boatload of friends with him. They sounded like they'd already started partying and Krissy knew that it wouldn't be long before their music was turned up and a cloud of pot smoke was slowly seeping through the crack in the drywall in her bedroom.

Linda Dynel

She agreed to be ready and watching for Dorian at the downstairs door at five-thirty sharp. He hated it when she kept him waiting.

Linda Dynel

Chapter 13

Once Krissy was behind the wheel, Meagan pulled out and waved goodbye. Spence pulled his car up next to Krissy's. "Just follow me. Once we're over the Skyway, we'll continue on Route 5 to ..."

"The Skyway?" Krissy could feel herself starting to panic again. She had very little experience driving on anything other than main roads and side streets. If she needed to go anywhere other than their immediate neighborhood, Dorian always drove her. And the Skyway was just exactly what it sounded like; a raised four lane thoroughfare. There were no soft shoulders and nowhere to slow down or stop if you needed to, and merging from the on and off ramps was done at breakneck speeds. Though it was a short stretch of road connecting downtown Buffalo to its southern suburbs, once you were on it, you were on it. Krissy was starting to feel a little light-headed. On her best day she didn't know if she felt like an experienced enough driver to manage the Skyway, let alone with the girls in the car.

Spence could see the panic on her face. "Kris, it's no big deal! It's just another road! It takes like three minutes. Come on, Kris, we gotta get outta here, now! Just follow behind me, O.K? I'll make sure that I keep sight of you at all times, so don't be afraid if you don't see me up ahead; I'll still see you. And if you get too far behind, I'll pull over and wait for you, O.K?"

"But you can't pull over on the Skyway ..." Krissy was trying hard not to start crying again. She'd come so far; she didn't want to fall apart over something as simple as short stretch of road.

"Kris, it'll be fine!" Spence's tone was kind, but firm.

Her mind was racing. She looked all around her, nervously scanning for a car that might hold a raging, screaming Dorian. And still, nothing. Krissy sighed; there was no other choice. She was going to have to drive over the Skyway, because she had to go.

"O.K," she nodded her head and rolled up her window.

Spence rolled his up, too, giving her a smile and a thumbs up before pulling out. She tried to smile back.

"Where are we going, Mama?" Anna asked from the back seat, her mouth still working the sticky caramel.

Krissy looked into her rearview. Grace was busy digging the last of the fruit snacks from their small blue pouch with the little cartoon dog printed on it, but looked up when Anna spoke, as if she'd been wondering the same thing.

Just as I rehearsed it, Krissy reminded herself.

"We're going to Uncle Spence's house. Do you know that he has two little boys; Ethan and Jared? They live there sometimes, too, and you girls are going to get to play with them and all of their toys! They're ..."

Anna interrupted her. "They're my cousins! That's what Meagan said! She said that the boys are my cousins and that she has a little boy too, and that he can be my cousin, too, if I want!"

"That's right!" Krissy tried to sound cheerful as she pulled out of the parking lot and onto Niagara Street, following closely behind Spence to the 190 on-ramp. Her stomach was flip flopping and she could feel herself starting to sweat.

She had imagined there would be bumper to bumper traffic on the 190, but it was well after morning rush hour so the only vehicles on the road with them were a potato chip delivery truck and an old pickup, and both of those were in the farthest left lane. Krissy slowed behind Spence's car and reminded herself to breathe. She was so deeply and profoundly out of her element, so consumed with fear, that she wondered if what she was experiencing could technically be considered a nervous breakdown.

"What kuzin Mama?" Grace asked as Krissy glanced in her rearview.

"Cousins, Gracie! Like Brittany and Connor!" Anna piped up.

Brittany and Connor were Dorian's sister's kids. Anna and Grace had only met them a couple of times, so Krissy wasn't surprised that Grace didn't remember them. Dorian didn't see his sister or her husband much. He thought they were the worst kind of people and the worst kind of Catholics. They'd continued to smoke and drink and party with their friends long after they'd had kids of their own. They worked steady, nine-to-five jobs; Nicole as a secretary and Vince as a plumber. They owned their own home and had two cars and invested in their retirement plans. They took vacations and spoiled their kids and lived life like most other married couples. They claimed to be happy. Dorian said that they were worldly creatures who needed worldly comforts. He said that they didn't know God the Father, that they didn't love God the Father, and anyone that didn't know and love God the Father didn't need to be anywhere near his precious daughters.

Krissy stayed behind Spence as he slowed to toss coins at the toll booth.

"What dis Mama?" Grace was always full of questions.

"This is a toll booth. It's ..." Krissy tried, but then knew she wasn't going to be able to do it. Normally when she had the girls in the car with her there was a constant running banter between the three of them. But for some reason as she pulled into the toll booth lane, a deep, cold fear had started to overwhelm her and she was having a hard time swallowing.

This is it, she thought as she tossed her quarters into the metal basket before speeding up to reach Spence's car. He was driving at just the speed limit, letting cars pass him. Krissy noticed that his head kept bobbing up as he kept watch for her in his rearview.

She was running away.

Krissy only had to drive for a minute or two before she could see cars up ahead merging onto the ramp that led to the Skyway.

Once she accelerated onto the ramp, she would be on her way to the South towns, a world away from their apartment and her job and her co-workers and everything that she held dear. Away from everything that was familiar in the closed, tightly controlled world that she'd lived in for so long. Then she noticed them, bright orange safety signs that read "Road Work Ahead" and "Single Lane Traffic". Her heart felt as though it were about to burst out of her chest. She was terrified of driving the Skyway when all four lanes were open, but to drive it under construction?

And yet she had no choice.

What if something happened, she was screaming at herself in her head. What if she couldn't manage whatever lay ahead on that scary raised roadway, and she crashed? What if something bad happened to the girls? Dorian would kill her. But first, he would tell her that she was a horrible, wretched sinner and a terrible mother and that the girls were injured or worse yet, killed, because she had to be a stupid selfish bitch who tried to run away from the one man that was put on this earth to discipline her and correct her and keep her on the straight and narrow path to The Kingdom. He would say that she'd thrown it all away, even sacrificed her own children, in order to try and gain worldly pleasures and possessions. He'd tell her that she was a whore and a harlot and the worst kind of sinner and that God the Father hated her and that she was going to burn in the Eternal Fires of Hell because she had killed her children.

Spence's directional was on to let her know that she needed to merge right, but cars were coming from another ramp and merging into her lane from the right. It was terrifying and Krissy looked in her rearview and over her right shoulder and then simply made the jump from one lane to another and was on the ramp behind Spence in a flash. Spence was slowing down and she slowed down, too. Traffic merged into her lane from what seemed like behind her and there were men in hard hats and men holding flags and great, thick concrete barriers on both sides of her and Krissy couldn't believe the situation she found herself in. Suddenly everything seemed ridiculous and unreal and she could see her hands on the steering wheel but she didn't think she could feel them anymore. Her foot was working the pedals but it seemed to be someone else's foot. She started to laugh as her car seemed to navigate itself past the work trucks and jackhammers and rebar sticking this way and that from the torn-up roadway. Krissy watched her right hand leave the wheel and turn on the radio. Her fingers pressed the forward button and the station switched from Catholic talk radio to on oldies station. Gloria Gaynor's voice came pumping through the car's front and rear speakers, *"It took all the strength I had, not to fall apart..."*

No way, Krissy thought, and she almost chuckled.

She was aware of Downtown Buffalo passing by her on the left, growing smaller in her peripheral vision, and tried to ignore the harbor just off to her right. Krissy had always been terrified of the water. But there were bigger, nastier things to be terrified of now, and she gripped the steering wheel even tighter and told herself that there was no way that her car would end up in that water. That was a crazy, unrealistic thought; just the overwhelming stress of the situation talking. Focus, Krissy scolded herself.

She wracked her brain for something else, anything else, to think about. High school was what came to mind. The high school she'd graduated from had been located just outside of Downtown Buffalo. She thought about the two years she'd spent there; about sneaking smokes in the bathroom and lunch with her friends at the food court in the Main Place Mall. Then she thought about college, and about how at one time she'd loved to dance. She'd loved pop music and driving aimlessly, just for the fun of it. She'd loved going to comedy clubs and concerts at The Aud and going out to dinner and partying with her friends, because at one time in her life she'd had friends. Not just co-workers, but real friends who called on the phone and came to the house and remembered her birthday and laughed with her and cried with her and shared memories with her. But now all she had was Dorian and her girls.

"I will survive! I will survive! Hey! Hey!"

The height of the Skyway was behind her now and an open Route 5 lay ahead. She passed long abandoned factories and dead looking grain elevators. There was a marina on the right that her mother's hoarder-boyfriend had taken her and Spence to a couple of times. They'd eaten hot dogs and French fries from the little lunch stand, and fed seagulls bits of dry bun and watched the sailboats drift on by. Krissy drove in silence and the girls were silent, too, all three listening to the music that was slowly enveloping them from the old car's more than adequate sound system.

Traffic slowed and they entered the Town of Lackawanna. They drove past block after block of the old Bethlehem Steel plant and the dozens of houses interspersed between the entrance and exit gates of the shuttered factory. Krissy started wondering just how much further it was to Spence's place; it felt like they'd been driving forever. Pizzerias and auto body shops and mini-marts lined the road on both sides, and then suddenly the Ford plant was up ahead and the road seemed busy again and there were large green road signs overhead announcing on-ramps and merge lanes and Krissy stared to feel panicky all over again.

She could see Spence's head bobbing up and down; he was keeping a close eye on her in his rearview again. Then he signaled left and she changed lanes with him and followed close behind and a minute or so later they slowed to a dead stop at a red light and Spence was turned all the way around smiling at her and giving her the thumbs up as he waited for traffic to clear so that they could turn right. Krissy breathed in and out deeply and tried to collect herself.

Chapter 14

The weather got cold and Krissy quickly realized that her apartment was almost unlivable. It was as freezing in the winter as it had been sweltering in the summer. There was only one functional heating vent and that was up near the ceiling in her bedroom, so her living area was cold even with the heat cranked way up. Without being able to afford a couch or any living room furniture, her place was mostly empty anyway, but spending every evening curled up on her bed watching her little TV was no fun either, since she still felt like she was sharing her bedroom with the guy next door. Then her first heating bill came and it left her feeling like she'd been punched in the gut; the bill for one month was more than her rent, and she had no idea how she was going to pay it.

Dorian warned her that if she didn't pay it, her heat would be shut off and the fuel company would sue her for the money. Krissy had no idea what he was talking about. They could just shut somebody's heat off? Dorian said yes, they could and they would, if she didn't pay. But couldn't she freeze to death in an apartment with no heat? Dorian said that the likelihood of her freezing to death was slim, but that yes, they would indeed shut her gas off. Big corporations like the fuel company didn't give a damn about the little guy. Krissy hoped that Dorian would offer to help her pay the bill, but when he suggested moving her out of her place in the middle of the night and in with - to avoid the whole breaking the lease problem - Krissy immediately said no. She didn't want to scam her landlord and she didn't want to not pay the bill. She hated her apartment, but didn't want to screw somebody else in order to fix her own problem.

Then two nights later she came home late after work and found Mickey sitting in the second-floor hallway. When she walked upstairs, she found that her apartment had been broken into. The door was wide open, having been kicked in so violently that it was not only off the hinges but the frame was torn from the wall, as well. Her TV was gone and her boom box was gone and so were all of the rolled pennies that she'd kept in a mug on the top of her fridge. Her underwear drawer had been rifled through and panties and socks and bras lay strewn across the beaten-up hardwood floor.

She'd walked right in, never thinking that someone could be lying in wait for her. Then that thought occurred to her but it was too late and she was scared and panicky and just wanted to be able to close her front door and cry in private. Instead, she picked up the phone and called Dorian. She was relieved when he picked up on the first ring, as he always let the answering machine pick up. He didn't even sound surprised when she burst into tears and told him what had happened; he simply told her to call the police.

Once a report had been taken and Dorian arrived, the landlord sent a workman over to fix the door. While they were waiting, Dorian suggested that she come stay the night at his place. He knew that she'd never feel safe in her apartment again, anyway, and there was no way she was going to get any sleep that night if she had to stay there. Once the workman left, Krissy put food and water out for Mickey and packed a bag and locked the door behind her before reluctantly going to Dorian's.

One night at Dorian's turned into two, which turned in to a week, and then into two months. He told her every day how much he loved having her around. Seeing her in the morning before she left for work; having her there when he got home from work at night. He was appreciative as hell that she'd decided to take on the task of cleaning and straightening his grungy little bachelor pad, and told her every evening how nice it was to have a home to come home to and not just a space filled with his stuff. They grocery shopped together and she did the laundry and the two of them seemed to fit together as cozy and comfortable as two peas in a pod. For a while Dorian was happy and cheerful and not at all as quick tempered and suspicious as he'd been before she moved in. When he asked her when she was finally going to break the lease and give up her apartment, she agreed with little hesitation. It seemed like the sensible thing to do, since she wasn't even living there. Besides, he reasoned, the two of them could really use the money.

She spoke with her landlord the next day when she made her daily trip over to feed and water Mickey. When he said that he'd let her out of the lease, but that he'd need to keep her security deposit, she agreed. She returned to Dorian's apartment that evening happy, her only concerns at that point being where they were going to put Mickey's cat box in the tiny efficiency apartment and where they were going to store all of her stuff. She'd taken everything she owned from her mother's house when she moved out, but she still had a small storage locker full in a friend's apartment building from when she'd left the Boy Next Door. As she started dinner, she asked Dorian if he'd ever rented a U-Haul truck before. They'd used her friend's pickup truck for her last move, but considering that they'd be emptying her apartment and her storage space this time, she thought it might be a better idea to just rent a U-Haul and get everything moved in one trip.

Dorian's reaction was like a slap in the face. He said he wouldn't have a dirty fucking cat box anywhere in his place, so she needed to find someone to take the cat. And whatever bullshit she still had in storage could stay there.

Krissy protested; she loved Mickey and couldn't believe that Dorian wanted her to just give him away. And her stuff was her stuff; she knew it was a pain in the ass but they were going to have to move it again. What was she supposed to do, just leave it all there?

That's exactly what they were going to do, Dorian barked back at her. He wasn't gonna have his whole place smelling like cat shit, so the cat wasn't even an option. And there was no way he was gonna bust his ass one more time moving all of her petty bullshit for no reason. It was either leave it all behind or find someone else to move it for her. But then again, he didn't have a storage space, so even if she found someone to move it for her there was still no place for her to put it, anyway.

Krissy started to cry. She'd cleaned out the closet in his bedroom. It was long and deep and plenty big enough for the dozen or so boxes that she kept in storage. Why couldn't she store her stuff in there?

Dorian wanted to know why she had to be such a whiney fucking baby; why she had to act like such a spoiled brat, and why the fuck did she think she could demand anything of him? Her name wasn't on the lease. His landlord didn't even know that she was living there with him. What if the landlord found out? Dorian said he wasn't sure what would happen. Maybe because her name wasn't on the lease, she wouldn't be able to live there at all. As a matter of fact, he suggested - suddenly subdued and strangely quiet - that maybe she ought to think about keeping her voice down. If the neighbors found out that she was living there and told the landlord, she could get them both kicked out; her for not being a legal tenant, and him for letting someone live with him who wasn't on the lease.

All at once Krissy wondered if she could sneak off after work the next day and talk with her old landlord; maybe set something up so that she could still keep her apartment. Living with Dorian suddenly seemed a lot less ideal than it had felt over the past two months. But then she started thinking about the unpaid fuel bill and how unsafe she'd felt living there and the pot-smoking guy next door.

Krissy reluctantly agreed to pare down the boxes to two or three; whatever she could reasonably fit in the hatch of Dorian's car. The rest she would leave behind. And she agreed to find a suitable home for Mickey.

That night Dorian took her out to dinner, then told her that he loved her for the first time in the darkness of his bedroom.

Grandpa Sam's mother, Lenore holding me, and Grandma Patty, 1969.

Me at twelve years old. The incident with Marcus happened within months of this photo being taken in 1981.

My high school graduation, with Grandma Patty and Grandpa Sam, 1987.

Dorian, 1969.

Linda Dynel

The bridal shower that my classmates hosted, 1993.

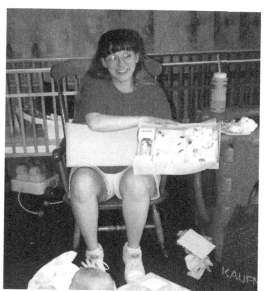

The baby shower that my co-workers hosted, 1995.

Leaving Dorian

Me with Anna Claire. Note the shortwave radio sitting on the table.

The house where Dorian strangled me the first time, nearly killing me in our kitchen. Kenmore, New York.

Linda Dynel

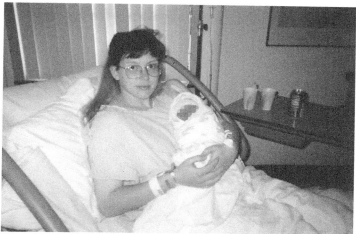

Me and Gracie. November, 1996.

The homeschool wall.

Leaving Dorian

The outdoor climber that sat in our living room.

Me with my girls, Easter, 1999. I was seriously considering killing myself when this photo was taken.

Linda Dynel

The building that we fled from in April of 2000. Kenmore, New York. We lived in the lower left unit.

Spencer's place, corner of Grover Place and Big Tree Road, Hamburg, New York.

Leaving Dorian

Linda Dynel

Chapter 15

Spence turned the corner off of St. Stephen's Drive onto Maple Road and then a block down turned onto a little dead-end street called Cottage Way. He parked just to the side of a gigantic old two-story house. Krissy parked behind him. She sat and looked around for a minute, trying to gauge her surroundings. She didn't know where she'd expected Spence to be living, but it certainly wasn't in a place like that. When he'd said that he had an apartment, she'd assumed that he was living in a building situated within a neighborhood, not at the end of a main road sandwiched in between two other busy main roads. The place felt wide open. Anyone driving past Maple on their way south would be able to see the house and all of their cars in plain view.

But who would be driving by, she tried to reason with herself. And besides, you had to drive so fast on Route 5 and on St. Stephen's Drive that no one would even be looking down that section of Maple, let alone be able to see her car as they went whizzing past. But then again, she fretted, they were only yards from the Niagara River; people fished and walked along the breakwall all the time. There was also a hot dog stand right across the street from the house; an eye-catching little place with red awnings and a large outdoor eating area. That could reasonably mean dozens and dozens of people walking right past the big old house on the corner and past her car parked right out front. And it wasn't like they were alone on Cottage Way, either; every family that lived in the eight or so houses that lined the interior of the street would have to pass her car at least twice a day. Krissy's stomach knotted tightly and she tried to breathe in and out slowly; it seemed as though she would be living the book definition of hiding in plain sight. If only there was someplace for her to store her car, she thought; someplace private and out of sight, at least from the main road.

Just behind the house on a narrow patch of grass there was a newer looking metal swing set. Krissy thought that patch of grass must serve as a yard for Spence's kids, and she thought that it would be nice to at least have that one outdoor play area for her girls, too. On the other side of the miniscule lawn was an old, saggy, two car garage. The windows of the garage were painted over on the inside. The outside of the garage had a concrete slab next to it and an awning, the type that people sat under in the summer time. Parked on the slab under the awning there was an old riding lawnmower partially covered with a blue plastic tarp. Piled all around the mower were large plastic bins jammed full to overflowing with what looked like tools and lawn ornaments and all variety of random stuff.

A junk pile, Krissy thought, much like what her mother's hoarder-boyfriend would have piled high and wide if he had been living there as well. Oh yes, Krissy suddenly remembered and sighed deeply; her mother.

Lenore was standing right there, on the short walkway next to the house that led into what looked like a mud room. She was heavy and old. Lumpy. Bleached blonde hair with plenty of gray growing in but still cut short to her head, just like she'd always worn it. She had her arms wrapped around herself in a hug, tightly holding a button-up sweatshirt closed over her protruding middle. She was squinting her eyes against the fine, misty rain that had begun to fall again.

Krissy took another deep breath. This was what her life had come to; she had to bring her children to live with the most malevolent person she'd ever known besides Dorian in order to try and save herself. She hated her mother but loved her mother and that mix of fear and loathing and desperation and love was making it difficult for her to reach for the door handle and get out of the car.

Lenore was smiling so genuinely that Krissy thought about smiling back, though she knew that Lenore's happy face wasn't intended for her. Lenore was smiling past her, at the girls. It gave her pause just for a moment, to try and believe that her daughters might finally have a family. A grandma who could love them unconditionally; spoil them and hug and kiss them and tell them how wonderful they were, even when they weren't acting wonderfully at all. Krissy had always wanted that so badly for Anna and Grace.

Even though her mother and brother had come to Alfie Toaster's only days before, sitting there staring at Lenore from the front seat, it still felt as though she were seeing her mother again for the first time. The two had come to the restaurant the week before to bring Krissy lawyer money. Spence had slipped her a long white envelope stuffed with cash, which she'd later duct taped to the underside of one of the file cabinet drawers in the rear of the management office. Lenore had hugged her and kissed her and cried as the three of them stood in the lobby of the restaurant, calling Krissy her princess and sobbing loudly that all she'd ever wanted was to have her daughter back in her life again. Servers and cooks and other managers were all choked up and some were crying right along with her. When Lenore and Spence finally left, everyone was overwhelmed at the reunion they'd witnessed and were telling Krissy how wonderful they thought it was that she and her mother had been able to reconcile, though no one except the other managers knew the real reason that her mother and brother had stopped in.

All Krissy could think was, "... as if...", though she smiled and thanked everyone and agreed that it was a blessing to finally have her mother back in her life again. Her guts were telling her otherwise, though, and she went home to Dorian and the girls that night praying that for as long as she would need to stay with Spence, that her mother could somehow manage to hold it together, if for no other reason than for the sake of the girls. Krissy knew firsthand the hell Lenore was capable of wreaking upon the hearts and minds of a couple of innocent little kids.

Krissy leaned back between the bucket front seats and unlatched the girls from their car seats. Then she spoke to them firmly, looking them both in the eyes. "That lady right there is my mama. She's your grandma. She lives here with Uncle Spence and your cousins Ethan and Jared. She's very excited to finally meet you, and I think she might even want to give you guy's hugs and kisses. You can call her Grandma Lee, O.K? Are you ready?"

Anna was positively breathless, scuffing her toes on the floorboards and barely listening to Krissy, she was so eager to get to that smiling old lady on the sidewalk. Grace looked back and forth from Krissy to Anna and then to Lenore. She simply nodded her head yes and dutifully followed behind Anna when Krissy finally got out and opened the door to release them into her mother's waiting embrace.

"Well, hello there, girls! Oh, my, how pretty you both are! Just like your mommy! Do you know who I am? I'm your Grandma Lee! Oh, I'm so happy you're both here! I'm so happy you're going to be staying with me and your Uncle Spencer for a while!"

Spence was right behind Krissy. "You alright?" he asked under his breath, shifting his gaze toward Lenore. Krissy nodded her head yes, though nothing could have been further from the truth.

It was no mystery to Spence how Krissy felt about their mother. Not long after she'd moved in with Dorian, Krissy had stopped speaking with her altogether. Dorian had encouraged that break, saying that Lenore would never change and that it would be best if Krissy cut ties and got on with her life. "Cut out the cancer," was one of Dorian's favorite sayings. Lenore had felt like a cancer on Krissy's soul for years before she'd met Dorian, so it had been easy to simply stop trying with her; to stop trying to get love and respect and acceptance. The only thing Lenore ever seemed to have to offer Krissy was bitterness and judgment and hurt, so cutting Lenore out of her life had seemed like the best solution at the time.

Now here Krissy was years later, allowing her two precious, innocent daughters to wrap their tiny arms around the woman who had verbally abused and neglected her. The woman who had wallowed in her own misery and self-pity until Krissy had felt invisible. The woman who had, in moments of overwhelming stress and extreme emotional upset, screamed at her daughter that she hated her life and wished she could end it all. The woman who had insinuated time and again that becoming a parent had been a mistake; a burden she wished she didn't have to bear. And yet here was that same woman, holding Krissy's daughters tightly and acting as though she'd just received the greatest gift in the world.

Maybe she's changed, Krissy thought, a jag of painful, searing hope stabbing into the center of her belly. Maybe she's mellowed over time.

"My princess, welcome back!" Lenore cried, releasing the girls just long enough to wrap her arms fully around Krissy's shoulders. Krissy hugged Lenore back in spite of herself, and tried to believe that things with her mother would be different.

Linda Dynel

Chapter 16

Once she moved in with Dorian, Krissy stopped thinking about breaking up with him and settled into a daily routine. She made the best of it, as living with him was easier than living by herself. His apartment, though sunless and airless and peripherally laden with roaches was not what she ever would have considered ideal, it did have a tub with a shower and a refrigerator that worked well and a small stove with four working burners, which was more than her last apartment had.

They got along pretty well when Dorian was in a good mood, and she learned how to act when he wasn't. She cooked and cleaned and worked. He ran his five miles a day and worked and they had sex almost every night. On Dorian's good days, Krissy felt useful and happy and loved. On Dorian's bad days, she tried to soothe him and be understanding and did her best to act in a way that wouldn't leave him even angrier.

They had fun on the weekends and he bought her new clothes and shoes so that she looked nice when they went out. He brought her to work and she met his boss. He took her to his mother's house for dinner and she met his sister and brother-in-law and niece and his elderly grandmother.

She hadn't spoken to her own mother in months, by design, but had accidentally lost touch with Spence, as well, because she never called the house anymore. She saw her extended family only sporadically, having lunch here and there with her grandparents when they were in town visiting from their retirement home in Florida, or with her Aunt Karen when she came into the copy shop that Krissy had started working at. But the visits became fewer and farther between as Dorian picked apart and criticized every interaction and conversation when Krissy came home after a visit and talked about what a good time she'd had. Pretty soon she wasn't speaking with her family anymore at all; they didn't have her home phone number and didn't know where she lived. Krissy knew without being told that Dorian would be very angry if she gave any of her family members his address or phone number, so she always made sure that they knew to reach her at work. But then she'd started to avoid their calls when they phoned the copy shop, and made excuses why she couldn't see them if she happened to be the one who answered the phone when they called. Her grandparents and aunt would ask vague but leading questions in order to try and figure out why it was that Krissy was keeping them at arm's length, but she always gave them equally vague answers and tried her best to seem cheerful and completely alright.

While Dorian was willing to accommodate Krissy's need to keep some of her extended family members in her life, her friends weren't even up for debate. Dorian didn't have friends, only co-workers, and Krissy was well aware that he expected the same from her. She also knew without him having to say it that as soon as she agreed to move in, she was also agreeing to remove her best friend Marnie from her life. He simply wouldn't tolerate their friendship.

The one topic Dorian was very vocal and definitive about was birth control. Within days of her moving in, he told her that he expected her to go on The Pill. It was the sensible thing to do, he demanded, as the sponge or diaphragm or whatever bullshit it was that she'd been using wasn't as foolproof as The Pill and he didn't want an accident. Krissy told him that she'd been on them in college and that they'd given her mood swings, leg cramps and terrible, debilitating headaches. She'd even had a girlfriend who'd died from a blood clot that doctors thought she'd gotten as a result of taking The Pill. Dorian said that Krissy was probably being melodramatic, and that she needed to make an appointment with a gynecologist.

He went with her to her doctor's appointment and sat close while she filled out the paperwork. He spoke under his breath to her the whole time they sat and waited for her turn, saying that it was probably a good idea not to mention that she thought she'd had problems with The Pill in the past, because the doctor might refuse to give her a prescription. She'd probably imagined those issues, anyway, Dorian said. Maybe she'd felt guilty for having sex with her college boyfriend and that's where the mood swings and the headaches had come from; just the stress from her guilty conscience. Krissy's palms were sweating as she walked into the examining room after her name was called. After speaking with the doctor for a few minutes about her medical and sexual history, Krissy mentioned that she was there for birth control. She thought about telling the doctor the truth about the problems she'd had, but then chickened out. She didn't want to have to explain to Dorian why she couldn't get the prescription. Instead, she decided to ask the doctor about something else that had been bothering her: she was noticing that sex had suddenly started to hurt, a lot. The doctor examined her and asked her if she was in a new or long-term relationship. Krissy said that she'd just moved in with her boyfriend, but that the relationship was fairly new. After asking with Krissy a bit more about Dorian, the doctor suggested that sex might be uncomfortable because she didn't actually want to have sex with him. The doctor told her that if she wasn't in a situation where she felt valued, loved and safe, that her body wouldn't respond the way it was designed to, and that sex would continue to hurt.

Krissy suddenly felt embarrassed and emotionally naked. She asked if she could get dressed and whether the doctor was going to give her the prescription or not. The doctor just looked at her for a moment, then nodded her head and said that Krissy could pick it up at the front desk before she left.

Then she looked at Krissy and said, "Good luck, honey," before closing the door behind her.

Krissy was visibly shaken when she met Dorian back in the waiting room. He looked at her with a mix of frustration and concern. "Did you get the prescription?" he asked, eyes narrowed.

"Yeah," Krissy mumbled, trying not to cry. She didn't want to be on birth control pills, but she also didn't like the feeling that the doctor had sort of stripped her raw. All she'd wanted was a prescription, not a lecture from some roly-poly, mother-hen type.

"So, what's the problem?" Dorian asked, stopping short before opening the front door of the office to leave.

"She said that sex might be uncomfortable because I don't really want to be in this relationship."

Krissy didn't know why she said it. The words just rolled off of her tongue, spilling out between the two of them like verbal vomit. It made her angry that the doctor would come at her like she had, though she was also sure that she'd only been trying to help and hadn't said what she'd said with any malicious intent. But still, to say those things? To mess with her head like she had? Krissy wanted Dorian to be mad, too. They would be mad at the doctor together. How dare she say that Krissy shouldn't be with Dorian; he was all she had. That thought alone made her even angrier, but it also made her want to cry. She felt angry and sick and sad.

"What?" Dorian barked as he slammed out the door, Krissy trailing closely behind him. "What are you talking about?'

"She said..."

"It hurts to have sex with me? You told her that it hurts you to have sex with me? Why the fuck would you say something like that, Kris?" Dorian's voice was getting louder as they walked down the busy Elmwood Village side street. His words hung in the cold air like vulgar balloons. Then he stopped short and turned on his heels to face her. "What the fuck did you actually say, Kris? What were the actual words you used? You had to have made her think there was something super wrong! Fuck! You were just subtly putting me down, weren't you? You were! Hey; was she good lookin'? You weren't attracted to her, were you? Maybe a little, 'oh, my bad boyfriend, and as long as you're down there'," Dorian's voice dropped to a low growl and he winked at her. "As long as you're down there..."

"Dorian! Stop! Why would you say something like that?" Krissy was still angry and the sting of the doctor's words still

Linda Dynel

prickled the back of her neck, but she suddenly wished that she hadn't taken the righteous indignation route. She wished more than anything that she'd just kept her mouth shut.

Dorian got in the car and Krissy got in the passenger side.

"You gotta watch what you say to people, Kris. You're too naive and stupid to realize how you come off. You made me look like an asshole to that woman! Thanks, Kris; thanks for treating me like shit." He kept his angry face on the whole way to the drug store, where he bought himself a bag of beef jerky. He ate in silence while they waited for her prescription to be filled.

Linda Dynel

going to get sick with this awful, stinky dog licking all over their hands and faces, and that will be my punishment for doing this ... for taking the girls away from the man who stands in the place of God the Father for them ... the girls will suffer for my selfishness ... for my iniquity ...

Her stomach was turning over on itself even as she was trying to push Dorian's voice out of her head, but suddenly Spence was standing behind her on the landing. He had a nervous little half smile creeping over his face. "I didn't tell you because I didn't think you'd come if you knew we had animals," he explained quietly as Lenore pushed past the dog, the girls scrambling in behind her.

"You didn't think I'd come if I knew you had a dog?" Krissy asked, trying to pretend that she was fine with it. "Why would I have a problem with the dog?"

"I don't know," Spence answered, sensing Krissy's discomfort but not able to pinpoint its source. "I wasn't sure how the whole religion thing was when it came to pets. We have a cat, too; that's not gonna be a problem, is it?" he asked hopefully, jamming his hands nervously into the front pockets of his jeans.

Krissy was noticing that her brother still seemed almost as jangled and upset as she was. His cheeks were pink and he seemed more breathless than he should have been from walking up the short flight of stairs.

"Of course not!" she lied, trying to laugh off her stress. After everything he had done for her and the girls so far, and for everything that was surely yet to come, she didn't want her brother to think for a moment that she was anything less than grateful. "There's nothing in the Bible or in the Catholic religion that says you can't have pets!"

Spence laughed a little too, but then he stopped and lowered his voice. "Yeah, but Kris, the way you've been living ... that shit that was all over your apartment ... that wasn't Catholic, Kris. I know I said this in the car, and I don't want to keep going on and on about it, but ... you do get that, right, Kris? That was just Dorian's screwed up version of it ... of religion or God or ... fuck, I dunno ..." Spence rubbed the back of his neck with one shaky hand. "I don't know how you did it for so long ... how you lived that way ..." He leaned over and tried to hug Krissy but she recoiled a little.

He pulled back and nodded his head, leaving his hands on just the edges of her shoulders. "I know; it's gonna be hard on you for a while. I got it. But I'm not gonna stop trying to hug you, O.K? I've been without you for all these years and I'm not gonna let you go ever again!"

Krissy smiled and deliberately gave him a quick squeeze before following him into the apartment. She watched like a spectator as her mother cared for her children, pouring apple juice into plastic tumblers and pouring out cheese crackers and pretzels onto napkins for a snack. Spence was helping Grace up to the table and Krissy absentmindedly leaned over and patted the dog's head.

She only wished it had simply been the hug that had bothered her. Unfortunately, it wasn't. The real problem was that she was trying to figure out how she was supposed to divorce a man whom she was still silently defending in her head.

Chapter 18

At Dorian's insistence, Krissy went back to school. She'd thought about going back to the University to study sign language so that she might work with deaf children, but Dorian said that she probably wasn't smart enough for that and why didn't she just go to the local community college and study child care instead? Community college was cheaper and it would take half the time to get a degree and she would practically be guaranteed a job considering all of the selfish, vain, feminist women who had kids and then left them to rot in daycare centers.

Krissy said she'd always wanted to work with deaf children, but Dorian said she was being selfish and that she was going to put them deeper into debt than they already were with his college loans by studying something that she wasn't smart enough to do and probably wouldn't be able to get a job doing anyway. Krissy said that they were her student loans to pay back and why couldn't Dorian understand that it was something she'd always wanted to do? Then Dorian said that he'd been with enough selfish, stupid women, and that if Krissy wanted to be a self-centered bitch, then she certainly could, but that he didn't have to put up with it. He said that he was beginning to think that she was just using him for the roof and the financial help, and that he wasn't sure anymore if he should keep investing himself in someone like her.

Krissy enrolled in community college, majoring in Early Childhood Education. She excelled in her studies and more than one of her teachers suggested that she consider transferring to a four-year school in order to complete a bachelor's program. Krissy always thanked them politely and said that she'd consider it.

In the spring of that year the two started going to Mass on Sundays. It was Easter time and Krissy wanted to attend an Easter morning service somewhere, like she had on and off when she was a kid. Her maternal grandparents had been practicing Lutherans who'd attended church regularly, but Lenore could usually only manage Christmas and Easter, and even that was sporadic at best. Some years she'd dress Krissy and Spence to the nines and make a huge show of attending, arriving early and mingling with the other parishioners in the church's hall lobby before planting herself and her children conspicuously in the front row, directly under the watchful gaze of the minister. Other years she'd throw their coats on over whatever they were wearing and make sure they arrived minutes after services had already started. She would hurry her children in through a side door, rushing them up the back stairwell of the church and into the balcony. Krissy remembered asking her mother once if they were Lutheran and Lenore had responded that God knew what was in their hearts, so they didn't have to *be* anything.

Dorian had been raised Catholic and had attended and graduated from parochial school. He told Krissy that while he didn't feel much one way or another about Catholicism, he wasn't going to bullshit around at a Lutheran church, so that if she was bound and determined to go to church on Easter, they might just as well go to the Catholic Church that was right around the corner from his apartment.

That first Easter Mass was an almost magical experience for Krissy; she felt strangely at home sitting in the cavernous beauty of the two-hundred-year-old structure, and though the pews were hard and it wasn't well heated, and even though she couldn't receive Communion like Dorian did, she felt a strong pull to continue attending. She liked the way the church smelled; like flowers and

Linda Dynel

furniture polish and candle wax and incense. She liked the rote prayers that almost sounded like chanting. She liked the genuflecting and the reverence that parishioners showed when they entered the interior of the church. She liked the statues and the artwork on the walls and ceiling, and the dozens of constantly burning candles. She liked the way the sun shone in through the stained-glass windows and made a myriad of jewel like colors dance along the ancient tiled floor and on the dark, oiled wood of the pews. The entire experience of attending Mass made her feel small and warm and comfortable. At home and at peace.

Krissy also liked the idea of 'priest', an unmarried man who was completely and totally dedicated to his faith and his church and who was called Father by everyone, young and old alike. She also liked the fact that the priest at this particular parish wore his collar all the time, and that he seemed to be respected in a different way than other men. This parish priest seemed removed from everyone and everything else in the world, and there was just something about that; something that Krissy could get behind. She could respect that man and take what that man said to heart.

After going to Mass with Dorian on and off for months, it occurred to Krissy that she belonged to the church in the most important of ways; that she was actually Catholic on the inside. For the first time since she was a small child and her parents were still married, Krissy felt as though she were part of a real family again.

In the fall of that year Krissy started Confirmation classes and continued to go to school full time and work full time. Once she was Confirmed that next Spring, she started gingerly bringing up the subject of marriage. Since working with the priest that had Confirmed her and learning more about her newfound faith, she'd come to the conclusion that it wasn't right that she and Dorian were living together without the benefit of marriage. She believed that if the two of them truly wanted to stay together, that marriage was their only real option.

Dorian protested. Marriage was a farce, he railed, and only led to heartache. And why get married if you weren't gonna have kids? And they weren't gonna have kids; of that he was absolutely sure. There was no way he was going to bring children into the world. Look around, he'd bark at her as he lifted weights while watching Sports Center on TV; the world was a disgusting cesspool and most of the people in it were scumbags who only looked out for themselves. How selfish to want to bring a kid into that! But Krissy continued to nag and Dorian continued to brush her off, though every once in a while, he acted as though he were considering it.

And then he lost his job.

It was a job that he loved and one that he'd worked hard at. It was exactly what he'd wanted to do and he was devastated at the loss. He blamed Krissy, implying that if he hadn't been so focused on her and their relationship that he might have seen the writing on the wall and noticed that his boss was displeased with him; noticed that his job was in jeopardy. Directionless and depressed, broke and miserable and tired of sitting around their empty apartment all day while Krissy was either at school or work, Dorian started attending weekday Masses. It was one or two days a week at first, an early morning Mass here or a noon Mass there, but quickly became an essential part of his daily routine.

It wasn't long before Dorian was spending whole chunks of his empty afternoons steeped in lengthy prayer. Krissy continued to work and go to school while Dorian looked for work after what he had taken to calling his Daily Obligation of prayer and attending Mass. After a couple of months of this new routine he started redecorating their apartment. He took down the two posters in the living room; one he had called the 'good girl' and the other the 'bad girl'. They were artsy prints of women that Krissy had always hated, not for any other reason but that she thought they were ugly and tacky. Dorian said that he liked them because they symbolized women in their purest forms. In their place he hung an image of Jesus and one of Mary. Next, he took down the poster of 'The Beast' from a TV show that he'd loved to watch. When he ripped the life-sized poster off of the wall, where it had been hanging behind a small occasional table where his phone sat, there were five or six roaches behind it that scattered. Dorian said that the roaches were symbols of hidden sin, of the filth and the degradation of the human soul. He said it was ironic that the poster - an image from the television, placed so close to the phone table - as the phone and the TV were two primary ways for the world to come into the house. He said it as though he hadn't been the one who'd hung the poster there in the first place. Within days Dorian had stopped answering the phone. Then he stopped watching TV, except for sports and news.

Krissy started attending Mass with him every morning because if she didn't, he would go on and on about the fact that they were living in sin and that the two of them had a lot of repenting to do.

Dorian got a new job just before Christmas. Soon after, he started talking a lot about an old girlfriend whom he'd lived with for a couple of years. They'd had a stormy relationship from the get-go, he explained, and certainly should never have stayed together as long as they had. He talked about her and her crazy, alcoholic dad and her younger sister and all of the weirdness that their relationship had brought into his life. Then around Valentine's Day, Dorian said that he thought that same old girlfriend might be stalking him and that he and Krissy should move. When Krissy said that she hadn't noticed anyone in particular hanging around, other than the usual cast of characters that lingered day and night on the street corners just outside of their apartment building, Dorian called her an airhead and said that she didn't see the details in things the way that he did. He was absolutely sure that this ex-girlfriend was stalking him and that she was bound and determined to do him and his property some sort of harm. Their break-up had not been amicable, he explained. She obviously harbored some very negative feelings toward him; probably hated him, in fact. He was sure that she and her violent family members were hatching a plot against him.

They were in a new apartment by the end of March. The place they moved to was an upper flat on a tree lined residential street off of a busy road, just outside the Buffalo city limits. The family downstairs had three kids and the neighbors next door and across the street had kids and Krissy started thinking more and more about marriage. She started bringing it up all the time. She didn't just want to be some guy's live-in; she wanted things to be right. She wanted to be married and she wanted to have kids someday.

Dorian told her that he'd prayed about it and had decided that even though he didn't want to, that he would agree to marry her for the sake of her immortal soul. That even though she'd lived with him for those couple of years and had willingly acted like a whore, treating her body like a piece of meat and a plaything and not at all like the temple that God the Father had deigned it to be, he understood that she was partially his responsibility now and that the only right thing to do for her was for him to take the hit and agree to get married.

While Krissy wasn't happy about Dorian's hesitancy, she was relieved that she was making her living arrangement right in the eyes of God. She asked a couple of her classmates, the only real friends she had left at that point, to help her shop for a smart, inexpensive dress for her big day. As word got around that she and Dorian were planning on tying the knot, her classmates secretly cooked up a special treat for her.

When she found out that they had decided to throw her a bridal shower, Krissy panicked. She didn't want to offend or disappoint her friends by telling them not to, but she also didn't want to have to tell them what Dorian's reaction might be. And how was she going to explain to Dorian that her friends knew that she was getting married? The only way that they could have known was if she'd told them. She was thrilled to finally be getting married, and though she knew that Dorian wouldn't be happy that she'd told her classmates, she still wanted to share her good news with someone. Contacting her family after such a long time away would not only have been close to impossible, it would have angered Dorian in a way that Krissy was sure would spell the permanent demise of any future plans. She was happy that her friends were happy for her, and she wanted Dorian to be happy about that, too.

Not letting all of the hard work her friends had put into her shower go to waste became incredibly important to Krissy. But where would she say she was going after class on the night that they'd planned, if she didn't tell Dorian the truth? And how would she sneak their gifts for her into the house afterward? She didn't drive the car, only Dorian did. It was beginning to look to Krissy like an impossible task, so she decided to take a bold step and simply admit to Dorian that she'd told her friends that they were getting married, and that she wanted him to allow them to throw her the bridal shower. It meant a lot to them, and it would mean a lot to her. She was shaking the afternoon she sat with Dorian and admitted that she'd told her classmates that they were getting married. She apologized over and over and begged his permission to attend the shower.

Dorian hesitated, and for a second Krissy thought she saw a bit of a smile turning up the corners of his thin lips. But then he simply shook his head and said he knew that he couldn't trust her and he truly didn't know why he was even agreeing to marry her, but that he guessed if she absolutely under no circumstances told them when and where the actual ceremony was going to be held, that he supposed he could allow the shower to happen. Knowing that her friends had said that they were going to show up and throw confetti after the private ceremony because Krissy had, indeed, told them when and where she and Dorian were getting married, Krissy prayed that they'd only been joking.

The shower was small and sweet. None of her classmates had much more in the way of finances than she did, but they all chipped in for pizza and wings and snacks, as well as a beautiful cake that Krissy didn't eat because it was Lent and she'd given up sweets as one of her sacrifices. They played silly shower games and each and every gift was given from the heart.

When Dorian finally arrived to pick her up, he acted pleased as punch over the whole thing, but the minute the car was packed with gifts and they were on their way home, he started making fun of her friends, the effort they'd made and the gifts they'd given. Krissy defended them and Dorian got louder. Krissy was hurt for her friends and for herself and started shouting back even louder. Dorian pulled the car over. He said that he'd dump her fat ass on the side of the road along with the trash that her whore friends had given them if she didn't shut up and show him some respect. Who the hell did she think she was, talking to him like that? He was going to be her husband in a couple of weeks, so she'd better decide whose side she was on; his or her whore friends. He didn't have to marry her. He could change the locks on the apartment that was in his name only, and she could get lost. End of story.

They were married in the tiny chapel in the back of the church where Krissy had been Confirmed. No one was invited to the wedding; not friends or family. Even the witnesses had to be provided by the priest. Dorian didn't want a fuss. He swore up and down that if he saw even one of Krissy's friends at the church that he would not go through with the ceremony. Krissy's family was entirely out of her life at that point and Dorian decided that since his family could not appreciate the true spiritual base that he was trying to build their marriage on, they were also unworthy to attend. They would ruin it, he said. Embarrass him. He didn't tell anyone from his family that they were getting married.

The priest who married them pushed for their families to be invited. Pushed for them to choose witnesses that they knew and cared about and who cared about them. But Dorian would not budge. One of the seminarians that witnessed their wedding rushed upstairs afterwards and hung out of a second story window, throwing colored confetti over them as they left the chapel. Dorian cringed, same as he had when the priest had insisted that he take a picture of the two in front of the altar as a keepsake. They ate Chinese buffet afterward, then went home and Dorian got lost in preparing for work the next day. Krissy laid on their bed and cried. She suspected she'd made a terrible mistake.

Within weeks of them getting married Dorian lost another job. They had no way to pay the bills. Krissy's full-time salary working as a clerk at a copy store wasn't enough to pay the rent and utilities and put food on the table. When Dorian suggested that she drop out of school and start working in day care right away, Krissy resisted. She hadn't worked full time and gone to school full time for two years to simply throw it all away and leave school without a degree. Dorian said that she was being selfish, and that if God the Father had wanted him to work that crappy job that he'd just been fired from, then he would still be employed there. Dorian demanded to know why Krissy thought she knew better than God the Father what was good for the two of them. Dorian said that he thought he was fired because he was Catholic and proud of it and that his beliefs made him unpopular with some of his more promiscuous female co-workers. He said that he'd probably been fired because one of them was interested in him, and that since he wasn't interested back, he must have ruffled some feathers and ended up on the short end of a losing proposition.

Dorian demanded to know why Krissy would want her husband to work at a job where he was being sexually harassed. Why couldn't she stop being so selfish and step up and take care of the bills for a change the way that he'd taken care of them when she was struggling and trying to find her way?

Krissy quit school a month before her internship was set to begin. Soon, she was working full-time at a day care center within walking distance from their apartment, as their car had died shortly after they were married. Dorian said that it was God the Father's way of telling them that they needed to be in the world but not of the world, and that they should start sticking closer to home in order to stay focused on Him. They started walking to a church a few blocks from their apartment every morning to attend Mass, and then Krissy would walk to work while Dorian stayed home and prayed and occasionally looked for work. He said that prayer was spiritual currency and that in actuality, he was contributing more to the family than she was since he was building a home for them in Heaven. He said that while working was important, that all Krissy was really doing was meeting their worldly, physical needs by making money. You give to Caesar what is Caesar's, Dorian would say to her, I'm going to give to God what is God's.

Krissy found out that she was pregnant in July of that year.

Dorian had decided right after they were married that they were damaging their union in the eyes of God the Father by using birth control and had demanded that Krissy go off The Pill. They would follow the practice of Natural Family Planning, he said. She would track her cycles and they would abstain when she was fertile. But when the time came for Krissy to tell Dorian no, that she was fertile and that she might get pregnant if they had sex, he would say that she was wrong, or lying, or said that she couldn't deny him sex. He was the husband and she was his wife. She was his property and he would do with her what he liked, when he liked. Just look it up in the Bible, he'd tell her over and over again. The wife shall submit to the husband. She had signed a document and swore to God the Father in front of witnesses that she would spend the rest of her life being subject to him.

Dorian insisted that when she wasn't at work or doing housework, that she pray lengthy hours as an Act of Contrition for treating her body as a toy and a thing and not as the temple that God the Father had intended it to be. He told her that he had learned through his extensive religious readings that the birth control pill was also an abortive agent. Dorian spent many evenings in anxious consternation, pacing and lecturing her that her sinful behavior before they were married may have killed any number of his precious children. He worried out loud that that the child that she was carrying might be born malformed or mentally challenged in some way as punishment for Krissy's previously sinful behavior.

Krissy was having a hard time sleeping and had no appetite. Her body ached and she wondered if Dorian was going off the deep end. She was almost three months pregnant when she lost the baby.

Dorian said that it was God the Father's way of telling her that she wasn't spiritually grounded enough; that her sinful nature was too deeply embedded in her for her to ever be a good mother. Dorian started saying that they never should have gotten married.

He got a new job, but one working with adults instead of kids. He hated the job and only worked it for a couple of months before quitting. Krissy was offered a better paying position at a nicer daycare center across town and took the position immediately. She took two buses to work every day and two buses home since they still didn't have the money to buy a new car. Dorian looked for work but spent most of his time praying and listening to religious programming on a shortwave radio.

In September of that year Krissy got pregnant again.

Chapter 19

The girls ate their snacks and Spence got back on the phone and wandered into another room. Lenore motioned for Krissy to take a seat at the table with the girls and poured her a cup of coffee. The mug Lenore handed Krissy was printed with words like "Pro-Choice" and "A Woman's Right to Choose". There was a Planned Parenthood logo stamped near the bottom of the mug.

Lenore smiled at Krissy; her eyes gleaming with satisfaction. "I hope things like this aren't going to be too much of a problem for you, Kris," her voice tight and sharp. "I'm still very pro-choice; very pro-woman, and so is Marnie. In fact, she's the one who gave me that mug, as a gift."

It was not so much a question as it was a statement. Krissy knew that and simply sipped her coffee in silence; she'd only been in the door five minutes and already her mother had thrown down a challenge. She decided to try and not let it bother her; instead, she thought about Marnie. The day that Lenore and Spence had come to Alfie Toaster's in delivery of her lawyer money, Lenore had mentioned that she had stayed in constant contact with Krissy's former best friend and that Marnie, too, had left her own husband after he'd beaten her so badly, she'd ended up in the emergency room. Lenore had told Krissy that Marnie was thrilled to hear that she was coming back and couldn't wait to see her again.

"And speaking of Marnie, I've got a surprise for you! She's leaving work at lunchtime today and driving in to see you!"

To be able to see Marnie again, after all the years apart? Krissy felt excited but also apprehensive. Dorian had hated Marnie. But why? Something about her hitting on him, maybe? Krissy didn't really remember. All she knew was that Dorian hadn't liked Marnie and so Marnie had to go. And he certainly wouldn't approve of her being anywhere near his children. But Marnie was apparently on her way and she would, indeed, be meeting the girls.

What was the harm? Krissy tried to reframe the situation in her mind. Marnie was coming, and she would meet the girls. So what?

Dorian wouldn't like it if he knew.

But he didn't know.

What if he found out?

But how would he find out? Who was going to tell him?

The girls.

Maybe the girls. Eventually.

The girls wouldn't be seeing him for a while; the restraining order he would be served with the next day would say three months. Three months no contact with his daughters. Three months no contact with Krissy, except for court appearances. Come within one hundred yards of Krissy or the girls and go straight to jail. Do Not Pass Go, Do Not Collect Two Hundred Dollars. Krissy's lawyer had said that he thought that was a reasonable amount of time. Enough time for Dorian to cool off while the divorce was being processed. Since they owned no property except for household goods and the car, the only thing they would need to do would be to divide up their few belongings and work out custody and child support. Just sign on the dotted line and be done with it. Easy. Divorced. So how would Dorian know that the girls were spending time with Krissy's old friend Marnie?

He's not omnipotent, Krissy told herself. He doesn't know where we are. He can't see me. He won't find me. He won't.

He won't.

He won't.

He might.

But what if he does?

The thought was like a punch to the gut and Krissy could feel her heart starting to pound heavy in her chest.

The car.

The back of the car was covered in Pro-Life bumper stickers. "It's a Child not a Choice", "You can't be both Catholic and Pro-Choice"; there were at least eight of them stuck on the rear of the old Celica. It was a distinctive vehicle, anyway, as you didn't see too many of them on the road anymore, but with those bumper stickers it was unmistakable.

Lenore put a plate of chocolate marshmallow cookies in the middle of the table, the kind that had been Krissy's favorite when she was a little girl. Immediately, Anna reached for one and Lenore's eyes flashed; her tone was sharp and laden with disgust. "No, Anna! Those are for Mommy!" The child drew her hand back as though it had been slapped. She looked at Krissy with a mixture of sadness and surprise.

A sharp prick of clarity pierced Krissy's heart as she realized all at once that she'd gone from the frying pan and into the fire, and that she'd taken her precious daughters with her. She thought about speaking up to her mother but then decided against it. She didn't know how long she and the girls would be living there, and starting an argument with Lenore so early on would be emotional suicide. Instead, she picked up a cookie and bit into it. She showed the remaining half to Anna. "See, honey, you don't like these; they're filled with marshmallow."

Anna hated marshmallow and stuck out her tongue in response to the half-eaten cookie. Lenore paused, and Krissy could see that she was trying to decide her next move. To Krissy's great surprise and relief, Lenore smiled. Then she rummaged in the back of a cupboard and pulled out a box of vanilla wafers.

"These were your mommy's second favorite cookie when she was your age, and I know you're going to like these!" she exclaimed much too cheerfully, giving each girl three of the small, round cookies. Both girls gobbled down their cookies and finished their juice and then Spence was back in the kitchen and munching cookies straight from the box before leading the girls into the living room to settle in for some TV time.

Krissy was finishing her coffee and trying to pay attention as her mom rambled on about how it was that she had come to live with Spence after he'd left Chloe, when Spence came in with his cell phone in his hand and announced that Meagan was downstairs. Lenore rolled her eyes and got up to rinse her coffee mug. Spence just sighed and shook his head, careful not to slam the front door behind him as he and Krissy made their way downstairs to start unloading the cars.

He started explaining sleeping arrangements as they jogged down the stairs. He said that while the girls were welcome to sleep in Ethan and Jared's bunk beds when the boys weren't there, that she and the girls were also welcome to share the king-sized bed in his room while he slept on the large leather sofa in the living room. Mostly, he explained, he slept at Meagan's house, so losing the bed wasn't a big deal for him at all. After they'd quickly unloaded everything out of Meagan's car into the mudroom, Meagan hugged Krissy goodbye and apologized for not coming up to visit.

"Your mom and I don't get along very well ..." she began to explain.

Krissy stopped her. "It's fine; she doesn't get along with anyone. Never has."

Spence looked at Meagan with a silly, wide-eyed expression. "See? I told you! It's not you!" Then he grabbed her and hugged her good-bye and whispered something in her ear that Krissy couldn't hear but didn't want to, anyway. With every passing moment, every interaction large and small, it was becoming crystal clear that living in the house with Lenore was going to be unnerving.

After unpacking the back of Spence's car, as well, Krissy took the black duffel bag from his trunk and gingerly laid it in the trunk of her own car. Then she and Spence hauled the boxes of clothes up into the attic while everything else went into the apartment. Once they were done, Krissy sat in the living room with him and the girls and tried to figure out what it was that they were watching; whether or not it had any redeeming social or educational value. She'd not seen regular network television, except for very late-night TV on the sly, for almost eight years. The girls had only seen Cartoon Network, and even that was only The Power Puff Girls, because Dorian had deemed that particular cartoon a good example for his girls. But now they were watching Spongebob Squarepants and were simply mesmerized. Krissy tried to figure out the point.

Everything was moving fast. Strange house, strange circumstances. People and TV and dogs and cats and unfamiliar foods and there were her two precious daughters sitting deep in the bulk of a stranger's couch, cuddled up next to said stranger. But the stranger was her brother and the couch was his own. He had an arm around each child and was holding them close, talking to them softly about what they liked and what they did for fun and how he was so looking forward to them finally getting to meet his sons, their cousins.

Spence got quiet and the girls melted into him. He must have been studying Krissy's face because after a few seconds he burst out laughing. Both girls looked up at him but then put their heads right back at his sides. Spence looked down at them, hugging them both close. Then he sighed, trying to hold back tears. "Welcome back to the world of the living, Kris."

Linda Dynel

Chapter 20

Krissy waited until she'd missed two periods to tell Dorian that she was pregnant again. She was afraid that if she lost another baby, he would spiral into a frenzy like the one she'd had to live through over the summer. She didn't think she could handle that again, while also trying to cope with the loss of another of her own precious children.

Much to her surprise, when she finally took the home pregnancy test and showed Dorian the two blue lines, he seemed genuinely happy. Almost as happy as he'd been when she'd miscarried months before.

When Dorian found yet another job and somehow managed to scrape together enough money to buy them yet another late model used car, Krissy still felt lucky that she'd been able to find a wonderful obstetrician within blocks of their flat. Dorian didn't like to be bothered leaving the house before he was ready to go to work in the late afternoons, and Krissy had to make all of her obstetrics appointments in the morning so that she wouldn't have to miss whole days of work. In the cool weather she walked, which Dorian insisted was good for her, anyway, since in his opinion she was putting on more weight than she should have so early in her pregnancy. As the weather got progressively colder and eventually snowier, Krissy simply took the bus the few blocks down the road to her doctor's office. It was in those quiet moments, walking in the sweet November chill or waiting for the bus in the muffled cold of winter, that she tried to relax and sink deeper into her ever changing body.

Dorian, however, went in the opposite direction. He borrowed stacks of books on pregnancy from the local library and read for hours on the topics of fetal development, nutrition and prenatal care. He started cooking all of her meals and monitoring her fluid intake. He drew up an exercise schedule for her and taped it to the living room wall, right next to a prayer schedule that he told her she needed to follow. His child was growing inside of her, and she needed to put forth her best effort to turn away from her own selfish desires and sinful ways and to follow his direction in order to be the best mother she could be. If she didn't do what he said, she would surely fail as a mother. She needed to remember that he was given to her by God the Father as a gift; that he was her spiritual advisor now, not just her husband. She had to get past her own worldly desires and remember that she was nothing without him and that unless she did everything that he told her to do, she would surely perish in the fires of Hell for refusing to obey.

Krissy paid attention to what Dorian said just enough to be able to agree with him and act as though she was going to comply, but then tried to focus solely on the tiny life growing inside of her instead. She was acutely aware that she was someone's mother now, and that she had a higher responsibility to consider. Her own needs, her own happiness and wellbeing, everything she was and ever would be, was directly affected now by this little person that would look to her for guidance and protection. She was second now; her child's happiness and wellbeing would always come first. She promised herself that she would never be like her own mother.

Dorian refused to allow Krissy to sign them up for Lamaze classes, opting instead to practice the labor breathing techniques at home with her on their living room floor. He told her that he didn't want her taking any drugs during the delivery; that she was to pray to the Blessed Mother for strength in order to get through the pain. He told her that if her faith was strong enough, she would be able to manage just fine. He told her that he'd read that pain medication could injure an otherwise healthy baby prior to delivery, and that he could not allow her to scar his perfect child due to her own human frailty and weakness. There would be no drugs during delivery, he told her over and over again, reminding her before every doctor's visit near the end of the pregnancy. He pressured her to make sure she let her doctor know that she was opting out; no drugs.

A month before she was due, her co-workers and some of the moms of the babies that she took care of threw her a little surprise shower. There were gifts and a lovely cake and though Dorian was surprised and angry when he picked her up that night because he had to turn off the car and help her load the many boxes and gift bags into the trunk, Krissy didn't care. The shower had been a wonderful surprise and had lifted her spirits in a way that she wouldn't have anticipated something like that could have.

And her spirits definitely needed lifting. She was becoming increasingly concerned that there was something mentally wrong with Dorian. She found that he was becoming more paranoid than he'd been in the past, and had also started what Krissy had labeled as 'magical thinking'. He implied over and over again that if he thought about something long enough and hard enough that he could manifest it. He was reading from both the Old and New Testaments for hours every day, and had started drawing direct connections between the readings and their own daily lives. The stories he read weren't just lessons with which to glean information; they were starting to become, at least in Dorian's eyes, commentary from God the Father on things that had happened to both Dorian and Krissy that very day. Or the day before. Or something that might happen the next day.

Dorian completely stopped watching television. His only link to the outside world came from listening exclusively to anti-government and religious programming on his shortwave radio. He said that since sin had come into the world through a woman, that the sin in his home should be symbolically cast out by a woman. One Saturday afternoon, in a dramatic home-cooked ceremony, he had Krissy cut the cord off of their television. He read scripture and they prayed before he tossed the TV to the curb, spitting on it before turning around and marching back upstairs to their apartment.

Leaving Dorian

As Krissy's pregnancy wore on, Dorian became increasingly more argumentative and mean. Being full of hormones and grumpy herself, her patience had started to wear thin. She felt isolated and sad and wished that her family was still in her life, not only for her new baby but also for herself. Whether it was out of frustration or impatience, instead of simply agreeing with him like she had for almost their entire relationship, Krissy started to yell back whenever he started a fight with her. They called each other names and hurled accusations like rocks, screaming at each other until they were both exhausted and hoarse. Then there were days that he backed off and they seemed to be on even footing again, but those days were few and far between.

Krissy labored for thirty-six-hour in order to bring Anna Claire into the world. She did it without drugs, and when the tiny pink bundle was placed in her arms, Krissy was shaking and exhausted but proud of herself. Once the staff nurses and doctors were out of the room, Dorian scolded her for not pushing harder. Anna Claire had been born at seventeen minutes past midnight. If only she'd tried harder, he'd told Krissy, his precious daughter could have been born on the Feast of St. Anthony.

Anna was a little over three months old the first time Dorian beat Krissy up. They'd been screaming and fighting, which had become an almost daily occurrence, as Krissy struggled to do what she knew was right for their defenseless daughter. She found herself trying to manipulate every situation, no matter how small, in order to keep her baby safe from a father that was clearly imbalanced and running his own flawed agenda. But months of constant battling had left Krissy frazzled and exhausted and near her breaking point.

She'd handed Anna to Dorian so that she might prepare formula. Though she breastfed Anna whenever she wasn't at work, her doctor had told her at her follow-up visit that afternoon that she had a urinary tract infection and needed antibiotics, and that she wouldn't be able to breastfeed while she took them. Dorian immediately became enraged when Krissy told him that she had a UTI. He accused her of all sorts of indignities, everything from not washing herself properly to getting the UTI on purpose so that she wouldn't have to be bothered with breastfeeding before and after work.

Dorian told her that if she wanted to be right in the eyes of God the Father, she would disregard doctor's orders and not take the prescription. Instead, she should pray for a resolution to the problem. He told her that she needed to offer her illness up to God the Father as a sort of blood offering; show God the Father that she trusted Him and loved Him and ask Him for healing. If she would only do that, Dorian insisted, then God the Father would hear her prayers and not only take the UTI from her, but He would also bless their family. Krissy could keep right on breast feeding when she wasn't at work, which Dorian insisted was the whole point. They both needed to remember that everything they did had to be focused directly on what was best for little Anna.

Dorian railed at her for over an hour while she talked over him, explaining, yelling and finally losing her cool and calling him names. She told him that she hated him and wished she'd never married him. She told him he was a fat piece of crap and that he was crazy.

Krissy was working full time and taking two buses in each direction every day since their latest car had died and Dorian had deemed it unfixable. She was practically supporting their whole little family all by herself again, as his part-time job paid little more than minimum wage. She was sick of being stressed out and exhausted all the time. She was in no mood to hear Dorian's accusations yet again, and just wanted him to shut up. She wanted to hurt his feelings enough to make him recoil and go into the other room; to lick his wounds and stay away from her.

Dorian was walking a fussy Anna back and forth between the back bedroom and the kitchen. He was lecturing and goading Krissy, though she had finally stopped yelling back and was trying to ignore him, even as he continued to get louder and more virulent. She really needed to pee again, and just wished that he'd stop needling her and go into the living room so she could sneak into the back bedroom and take one of the Ciprofloxacin that were in the little brown prescription bottle in her purse.

"You've got to choose," he kept on relentlessly, patting Anna's back as he walked slowly from one room to another. "Is it going to your will, or God the Father's? Is it going to be ..."

"Shut up!" Krissy screamed at Dorian, slamming the canister of powdered formula down on the counter. "Just shut the fuck up! I'm sick! It's not my fault, and I'm not gonna let your crazy ass keep me from taking the medicine that I need to get better!"

And then for some reason, she took a step forward and pushed him. It wasn't very hard, she just shoved him with one hand by his right shoulder. At five foot seven she'd always been dwarfed by his six-foot two frame, but since the pregnancy, his weight had shot up even more than hers, and he hadn't taken any of it off. He easily outweighed her by more than one hundred pounds.

It was in that moment that she saw something change behind Dorian's eyes. Something snapped, or gave way. It was in that brief second, even before he'd side stepped her and quickly strapped Anna into the baby seat that was perched atop their kitchen table, that Krissy realized that something very bad was about to happen.

He was on her in a flash, grabbing her around the neck and squeezing his fingers into her flesh, pushing his thumbs firmly into her windpipe. He was squeezing with enough force to stop the air to her lungs to a whisper. She could feel herself struggling to breathe as her hands clawed at his arms and face uselessly, but what was scarier than the thought of suffocating to death right there in her own kitchen in front of Anna Claire was the look on Dorian's face. It wasn't angry so much as it was curious. It was as though he'd thought about that moment for a very long time and was trying to weigh what he must have thought it was going to be like to strangle her as opposed to what it was like in the actual doing.

Krissy started to feel weak and lightheaded and stopped struggling. She could feel her legs starting to go out from under her. That's when Dorian let go of her neck. In one efficient move, he had her left arm twisted behind her back and was slamming the side of her face into the counter with the palm of his hand. Uncapped bottles full of hot water and powdered formula went spilling here and there. Krissy could feel the steaming water and the grit of the powdered milk splashing into her eyes as he slammed her head into the counter over and over again.

He called her vile names and then snatched her up, grabbing her by the front of her t-shirt. He screamed in her face and she could smell his sour breath filling her nostrils. She could feel the foamy spittle spray against her nose and mouth. He hated her; she knew it for sure. He hated her but he also hated himself and he hated their life and Krissy thought that if he'd had a gun in the house that he might have killed all three of them right then and there; been done with the whole useless endeavor of life as he knew it.

But he didn't own a gun.

Instead, he threw Krissy to the linoleum floor. Then he walked to the sink where he washed his hands and mopped his own sweat-soaked face and neck with a dish towel. Then he unlatched a screaming Anna from her baby seat and started patting her heaving back as though nothing had happened. He mumbled something about cleaning up the mess before walking Anna into the living room.

Krissy sat up and watched the swinging door close behind him. Her throat was raw and her face was bruised and her whole body ached, though she knew that the physical damage she'd sustained was the least of her worries. As difficult as their relationship had ever been - in the last three minutes - everything had changed.

Linda Dynel

Chapter 21

Krissy just sat there in the living room with Spence and the girls, allowing her body to sink ever so slowly into the bulk of the leather couch. Normally, she'd have a child on either side of her; Anna sitting next to her but not touching her, Grace flopped over her lap while they watched a religious cartoon on videotape. But here she was sitting by herself while the girls sat across the room with Spence, Anna snuggled up right next to him, same as Grace. Krissy took a long look at her older daughter and sighed deeply; she had no idea how she was going to raise that child.

Anna Claire was indeed Daddy's Girl. He had named her and had been out of work or underemployed long enough during her infancy that he'd been her primary caregiver until she was almost a year old. Daddy and daughter had a relationship that Krissy was simply not a part of; Dorian had made sure of that. They had their inside jokes. They had their secret language. And when Dorian made fun of Krissy in a particular sing-songy, little kid voice that he used only with Anna, she followed right along and made fun of Krissy, too.

"Mama-Moo!" Dorian would prod and needle Krissy about her weight all the time. "Right, Anna? We love Mama-Moo!"

"Mama-Moo!" Anna would sing back to her Daddy, her face glowing with the love she felt radiating from him.

Then Dorian would smile slyly at Krissy as if to say, "Gotcha!"

Grace, on the other hand, was Mama's Girl. Krissy had lost her own job halfway through her pregnancy with Grace, though luckily unemployment had allowed her a little breathing room until she delivered. She didn't go back to work again until Grace was eight months old, and even then, it was working nights as a shift manager at the Alfie Toaster's down the street, so Krissy had all day, every day, to spend bonding with baby Grace. Dorian had somehow found a full-time day job right after Grace was born, so Krissy was able to keep her job working nights in order to stay home with the girls during the day.

Anna had been an easy baby, but as soon as she was able to speak, she'd started talking back and second-guessing Krissy. Most times she simply ignored Krissy if Dorian was home. Krissy always tried to stay focused and firm, every day trying to loosen the hold that Dorian had over their older daughter. It had been tough, and it would remain so, Krissy was sure of that. Spence had already raised his eyebrows a couple of times after Anna had spoken to Krissy in a way that seemed way too mature and almost disrespectful, but Krissy had immediately tried to brush it off. "It's fine. She doesn't know any better, and she doesn't really mean anything by it."

Spence hadn't been convinced. Anna was tall and mature for almost five, and when she looked at Krissy, Spence was sure he saw a bit of contempt for her mother in the child's otherwise happy, sparkling gray eyes. It was Dorian's doing, Spence knew; a seed of Dorian's own hatred for his wife that he'd carefully planted in the child's heart. The thought made Spence shudder. He'd only met Dorian a couple of times, but that had been years before, when Dorian and Krissy had first started dating. He didn't really know the guy at all, but he was sure that the man was pure evil. What kind of a guy hits a woman, for goodness' sake? Who tortures his wife emotionally and physically, lives like a religious hermit, and actively tries to poison his kids against their own mother?

As the cartoons wore on, Krissy's body began to relax and her eyes started to close. Even as she was drifting off, a thought came to her and her eyes fluttered back open. What time was it? The cable box said twelve-thirty.

If she were home, she would be finishing lunch with the girls, cleaning up and getting them ready for midday naps. Their mornings were spent doing academics; letters and numbers and reading. Krissy used a primary school curriculum from the nineteen forties designed by a Roman Catholic press, which Dorian had found online and ordered at a considerable expense.

After lunch and naps, it would be time to run errands, whether it be walking the girls to coupon shop at a local pharmacy or up the street to the local AmVets to peruse the many racks of used clothing in hopes of finding something suitable for her and the girls. Then home for Bible reading, after which Krissy would pop in a religious cartoon video to settle the girls while she made them dinner. Dorian would come home just in time for Krissy to leave for her shift at the restaurant.

Money shouldn't have been tight but it always was. Dorian took care of the bills and the bank account and made sure that a full third of their income went to religious charities, some in the States and some overseas. What little money they had left went to the basics, though Dorian always made sure that he had brand new clothes and shoes. He explained away Krissy having to shop for herself and the girls at secondhand shops as simply a matter of practicality; she wore a uniform to work and they were kids. No one cared what the three of them looked like. As long as Krissy kept herself and the girls neat and clean, what was the harm in buying used clothing? She needed to get her vanity under control, he'd lecture her. Who was she trying to impress, anyway, he'd rail; who did she need to look so good for? He, on the other hand, needed all the newest styles because he worked in the real world every day, without the benefit of a uniform. He told her to suck it up; to stop acting like a selfish whore.

Anna stopped needing a nap right after she turned four, but when Krissy tried to talk to Dorian about it in order to try and figure out a way to modify their daily schedule so that Anna might be allowed to read quietly to herself in bed instead of constantly chatting and goofing and keeping Grace awake, Dorian scolded Krissy for being lazy. He told her that if Anna wasn't tired enough to take a nap, it meant that she wasn't getting enough mental stimulation during the day. He berated Krissy for being a bad mom and a lazy teacher and told her that if she couldn't or wouldn't start working harder with Anna that he just might consider quitting his job and staying home with the girls during the day in order to take care of the homeschooling himself.

Nervous about changing Anna's nap schedule herself but even more nervous about stirring the pot any further with Dorian, Krissy started leaving picture books and coloring books and crayons on the end of Anna's bed right before nap time. She didn't mention them to Anna as she settled the girls down for nap, just kissed them both goodnight and turned on their lullaby tape and told Anna to be quiet so that Grace could sleep. It didn't take long for Anna to figure out that once Grace was asleep, she could read her books and color by herself without having to share her things with her sister. Within three days, Grace was napping peacefully for two solid hours and Anna didn't have to be scolded anymore to be quiet and stay in bed. As far as Krissy knew, Anna had never mentioned the change in her nap routine to Dorian, either.

Maybe there was hope for the two of them, Krissy thought as her eyes closed again, Spongebob Squarepants droning on in the background. Maybe she and her Anna Banana might someday be able to find a middle ground, a peaceable place where Anna could love both her and Dorian equally.

The phone rang, and Krissy just about jumped out of her skin. It was him! She was sure of it! Dorian had found her and he was calling to say that he wanted his daughters back! Oh, God, she thought frantically, sitting straight up on the couch, what the hell was she going to do? Tears welled up in Krissy's eyes.

"She's on her way!" Lenore screeched from the kitchen before thundering into the living room. "That was Marnie! She'll be here in half an hour!"

Krissy crumpled back into the couch. The tears that had been hovering in the corner of her eyes fell, rolling gently down her pale cheeks. Why had she thought that it was Dorian, she wondered. Spence was looking at her with a mix of concern and apprehension.

"Kris, I told you we have an unlisted number." Both of the girls were looking at her, too, but neither seemed concerned. They'd seen their mama cry hundreds of times.

Linda Dynel

"I know," she stammered, wiping at her cheeks with the palms of her sweaty hands. "I just ... I dunno ..."

Krissy got up and headed toward the bathroom; she wanted to be alone. Once she'd composed herself, she told Spence that she was going downstairs and asked if he could please keep the girls upstairs with him. He agreed, pulling out a board game and setting it up on the large square ottoman in the middle of the room.

Grace was surprisingly willing to let Krissy leave, once she was reassured that if she stood on the shorter couch and looked out the window that she would be able to see her mama down on the street below.

"If you wave and I'm looking up, I'll wave back, O.K?" Krissy cooed to the tiny child, stroking the curly brown hair that hung well past her waist. Grace nodded, then sat down on Spence's lap for a rousing round of Connect Four.

Krissy fished around in the kitchen drawers until she found both a steak knife and a box cutter. She was going to try and remove those very distinctive bumper stickers from the back of her car. Plus, Marnie was on the way, and she didn't want their first hello in so many years to be tainted by her mother being a part of it.

Lenore had reminded Krissy over coffee that morning that she and Marnie had become close friends over the years. So close, in fact, that she'd become somewhat of a surrogate mother to Marnie. "She's my daughter now, too, Krissy. I hope you can understand that."

Lenore had said those words with such venom, such vitriol, yet with such a sweet smile on her face that Krissy knew beyond a shadow of a doubt that her mother had not changed one bit in all of the years that she'd been away. Lenore was still as vicious and manipulative as she'd always been, though now she would be even worse to Krissy because she felt justified in her anger toward her.

Krissy had abandoned her, even after Lenore had sacrificed her whole life for her children. Wasn't that what she'd always said, that she'd sacrificed everything; her time, money and her personal life - *everything* - for Krissy and Spence? It was complete and utter bullshit, and all of them knew it, but Krissy could be blamed for acting badly now, too, having essentially disappeared for almost a decade. This indisputable fact gave Lenore, at least in the old woman's warped mind, emotional leverage over her daughter. And it wasn't a newsflash to Krissy that her mother had always harbored a very specific seed of contempt toward her, though she knew that it wasn't due to anything that she had ever done or said. No, Krissy suspected that her mother had been tending that poisoned seed since well before she was even born.

Lenore had been absolutely miserable near the end of planning her wedding to Buzby. So miserable, in fact, that her dad had started wondering if he should keep pushing as hard as he had been for the marriage to take place. Yet when he told Lenore that she didn't have to marry Buzby if she really didn't want to, essentially backtracking on everything he'd said up until that point in an effort to get his lazy, immature daughter married off and out of his house, Lenore hadn't been able to take him up on that very tempting offer as she'd already realized that she was pregnant. Since she was acutely aware of just exactly how her parents would handle news like that, she kept quiet and married Buzby, delivering Krissy seven months later, much to the chagrin of her perpetually mortified parents.

Krissy knew that in Lenore's estimation, the birth of her daughter had ruined her life. She had always suspected that Lenore would spend the rest of her life, deliberately or inadvertently, making Krissy pay for it. Sitting there at the kitchen table with Lenore earlier that morning, she was more convinced than ever that her mother was still not done with her.

The rain had stopped and as soon as Krissy got down to the car she looked up at the window. Sure enough, Grace's cherubic little face was pressed against the glass. Krissy could see her daughter's tongue licking circles on the pane as the child gazed intently into the distance, clearly entranced by the Niagara River that flowed just on the other side of Route 5. Krissy waved both arms to try and catch her daughter's attention. After a moment, Grace saw her and frantically waved back, jumping up and down on the couch. Someone must have called her for her turn, though, because in an instant Grace turned away from the window and without a second look in Krissy's direction was gone from view. Krissy sighed; it was strange to have help with the girls.

She immediately realized that the steak knife was largely useless for peeling, so she tried the box cutter. Nothing. Frustrated, she started to wonder just what the hell bumper stickers were made of. She stood up and brushed gravel from the knees of jeans that she suddenly realized were far too big for her, and was about to venture into the junk pile that sat under the awning next to the garage to see if she might find anything sharper than what she was currently working with when a brown SUV pulled onto the street and parked behind her car. Krissy caught her breath as the door opened. Just like that, there she was; Krissy's oldest and dearest friend, materializing before her eyes, almost like magic. It was Marnie.

Linda Dynel

Chapter 22

Sex with Dorian had never been what Krissy would have labeled as fun. Or exciting. Or pleasurable. It was more of a chore or an obligation that needed to be fulfilled. Part of the deal. A toll to be paid for remaining in the relationship with him. She had been raised to believe that sex was either something unpleasant that a woman simply got through in order to appease her partner, or something that could be fun and extremely gratifying but only if the woman was a 'bad girl' and able to act like a whore.

Krissy was a sounding board for her mother starting at the tender age of nine, so she grew up hearing all about her mother's personal life; all of Lenore's crabbing and moaning over having to listen to some guy's sob stories after his five minutes of bouncing up and down on top of her when Lenore tried to be a 'good girl', and all of her bragging and showing off of the hickeys and bite marks and mementos from fancy restaurants and bars when she didn't. Either way, men never seemed to call Lenore back.

Krissy decided very early on that she would rather try and manage a relationship by being a 'good girl' than end up having to drag herself home in the early mornings, hung over and exhausted, with only a fancy collectible glass and a ripped pair of stockings to show for it. She decided that she wanted to be the kind of girl that men wanted to call back.

When Dorian and Krissy first met, he'd claimed to have watched a lot of porn and to have experimented with plenty of women. He knew what he wanted in bed and if Krissy resisted, he implied that she was prudish or frigid. He wondered out loud what was wrong with her, offering to go to the library and look up real-life case studies of sexual dysfunction for her so that she could educate herself about what he claimed were her very real issues.

Not wanting to hear his constant innuendo and feeling like a failure for not being able to get as wild and turned on as the other women he'd claimed to have been with, Krissy decided that it wouldn't be the worst thing in the world to try and accommodate him. She had her own ideas about sex and what it should mean and how she wanted to feel while engaged in the act. Since Dorian was the guy she was with, she tried time and time again to please him while also trying to make it a pleasurable experience for herself, as well. Most times, she failed at both.

Once they were married Krissy felt as though there was no turning back; they'd been married in the Church and that meant forever. It was a monumental step that she thought would somehow magically change their entire relationship; improve it somehow, make them closer and more compatible. She thought becoming Dorian's wife would somehow make him love her more. Almost immediately, she'd realized that simply wasn't the case and was never going to be.

It was sometime shortly after this disquieting realization that Krissy became adept at what she'd started thinking of as 'going away'. She would steel herself when Dorian started pawing at her, and soon her mind was somewhere else. Her body was moving and she was moaning and saying whatever it was she thought he wanted to hear, at some point faking a big finish, but she learned over time that in order to get through the process and keep Dorian happy that she needed to make sure that she was not really there at all. Often times, she felt like she was floating above the two of them, though other times she simply went away. She'd think about something entirely different; try to remember the details of a movie she'd seen when she was a teenager, or a fun time she'd had with friends, years before. Dorian never seemed to catch on that she might actually be faking interest and he certainly never seemed to notice that she was actually disgusted by him, though Krissy didn't think he was usually paying much attention to her, anyway. As long as she went through the motions and acted as though she was enjoying it, Dorian never complained.

After months of this 'going away', Krissy started to notice a disturbing fact; most times her body continued to respond to Dorian, even though her mind was mostly shut off. Then one afternoon she was listening to a strictly off-limits radio program while Dorian was at work and she heard a psychologist talking about the guilt that rape victims sometimes felt when their body responded in a way that they hadn't wanted it to during the attack. All along Krissy had thought that maybe somewhere deep down she really was attracted to Dorian; that maybe she actually did like everything that he was doing to her and the disconnected and impersonal way that he treated her. She'd started praying over and over for some resolution to that nagging fear. After hearing what the radio psychologist had to say, Krissy understood and felt better. She also started listening to that radio program on the sly every chance she got.

She also prayed that God the Father would make her marriage fruitful. She believed Dorian when he told her that God the Father had created marriage for the sole purpose of bringing new life into the world so that new souls could ultimately be brought into The Kingdom of Heaven. She wanted nothing more than to be a mother, and hoped that maybe Dorian was right, that if she could be good enough and holy enough and right enough in the eyes of God the Father that they would be blessed with a baby as a reward for being His good and faithful servants.

It was right after Anna was born that Krissy took the two most severe beatings she would endure during their marriage; the first when he almost strangled her to death in their kitchen, and then a second only a few months after that. Both times she'd been left heavily bruised around the face and neck and was so sore that she'd had a hard time getting around afterwards. She couldn't leave the house for days, and Dorian ended up having to run all of their errands and do all of the laundry and shopping. It didn't take long for him to realize that if he kept marking his wife in places where people could see, he would continue to be inconvenienced and his free time severely limited. In order to compensate for the frustration he felt over having to curb his behavior toward his wife, the emotional battery Dorian inflicted upon Krissy ramped up to proportions that she would have never thought possible. Name calling and vicious verbal attacks regarding her family, her spiritual state and her capability as a mother were inflicted upon her on a daily basis, sometimes multiple times a day. Dorian questioned her sexuality, her mental state and her fidelity to him. He accused her of secretly worshiping Satan and plotting to harm him in his sleep.

Eight months after Anna was born Krissy found out that she was pregnant again. Two months after that she lost her job. Two very good things came from those two monumental happenings; Dorian tried in earnest to find a full-time job that he might want to stick with, and he stopped insisting that Krissy have sex with him when she said that she was in the fertile part of her cycle. But as with all things that had to do with Dorian, for every good outcome there was an equal or even greater bad one. More hours spent working a job he would learn to hate and fewer opportunities to exhibit his mastery over his wife left Dorian feeling weak, his masculinity compromised. Soon, violence against Krissy once again became the focal point of his days.

Over time, Krissy stopped looking at her belly and chest, upper arms and thighs, when she got in and out of the shower. Since she couldn't seem to stop herself from studying the bruises, counting them and checking on the healing process, she simply stopped looking at her body altogether. She would only look at herself once she was dressed, and even then, she was ashamed at what she saw.

Chapter 23

Marnie hadn't changed a bit, she was still just as petite and thin as she'd ever been, with longish dark hair and a smile that had always reminded Krissy of a jack-o-lantern. She tossed her cigarette into the grass and exhaled a stream of thick white smoke through her nostrils as she walked toward Krissy with long, deliberate strides. Krissy didn't know what she should say, so she said the first thing that came to her mind that seemed lighthearted and cheery. "Oh, my goodness, look at us! We're old!"

Marnie chuckled. "Speak for yourself! I'm not old!" Then she grabbed Krissy up in her short, thin arms and hugged her tightly.

It should have been awkward and uncomfortable, the two friends seeing each other again after so many years, but it wasn't. They stood in the gravel on the side of road for a minute or two and talked, then Marnie suggested that they go upstairs.

"My daughter! How are you?" Lenore gushed, pushing past Krissy to give Marnie a hug and kiss though she was barely through the door. Spence was standing in the archway between the living room and the kitchen with his arms folded over his chest. He wasn't smiling, and when Krissy gave him the 'What's wrong?' face he simply rolled his eyes.

"Hey, Lee," Marnie obliged the old woman, but just as quickly broke free of her grasp, setting her purse on the table. "Wow! Our girl looks good, huh?" she said, rubbing one of Krissy's arms with a cool, light touch.

"Do you want some coffee, honey?" Lenore asked, ignoring Marnie's comment, as well as Krissy. "I baked some of that honey wheat bread last night that the boys like so much; do you want a slice with some apple butter? It's the batch I made it with the apples that we picked with the boys last September. And, oh," Lenore stopped, suddenly realizing that Marnie had come alone. "Where are my boys?"

"I decided to leave them home with Bill. It was too much of a pain in the ass to drive home and get them, and I was already on the way. Besides, there's plenty of time for all that; I just wanted to get here and see her with my own eyes!" Marnie smiled broadly at Krissy as she sat at the spot where Lenore had set her a coffee mug. It was the same mug Lenore had given Krissy earlier in the day.

"That's the mug you gave me, see?" Lenore chortled, and now it was Marnie's turn to roll her eyes as Lenore took a large bread knife from the wooden block on the counter and started to cut a thick slice off of a tall brown loaf.

Spence stepped fully into the room at that point with the girls on either side of him. It seemed to Krissy that he was very nearly protecting them. Marnie suddenly realized that they were standing there and turned to looked at Krissy's daughters, wiping a tear from her cheek.

"You must be Anna," Marnie almost whispered, her joyful surprise clearly mixed with sorrow, "and you're Grace, right?"

Anna nodded her head vigorously and stepped right up for a hug from the stranger when Marnie held her arms out. Grace, on the other hand, hugged one of Spence's legs tightly with both arms, refusing to let go or even look at Marnie. Spence looked smug and strangely satisfied.

"Hello, Spence," Marnie said, very deliberately trying to catch his eye.

Spence was just as deliberate in his unenthusiastic hello. Then he reached out and took Anna's hand and announced, "I'm taking my nieces across the street for lunch and ice cream. Where's their coats, Kris?"

Krissy wasn't sure what was going on between Spence and Marnie, but was just as glad that Spence had the wherewithal to get the kids out of the house since her old friend had arrived. Lenore seemed to be winding up, and Krissy knew what that meant; pretty soon she'd be using her loud voice and cursing. Soon she'd be off on inappropriate tangents and talking about things and people and emotions and circumstances that weren't relevant and didn't make any sense. This was the day-to-day, normal Lenore that Krissy remembered; not the polite, demure, completely coherent Lenore that had visited Alfie Toaster's, impressing the staff and customers alike with her genuine care and concern for her daughters and grand-daughters. This was the Lenore that Krissy had grown up with.

As soon as the girls' coats were on and Spence had them out the door, Marnie refused to give Lenore audience and the old woman quieted down and sat and listened while the two friends caught up. Krissy spared no detail in describing what she'd gone through with Dorian, and Marnie gave her the quick version of what she'd gone through with her first husband, Mark. Krissy was devastated. They'd all gone to college together, she and Marnie and Mark. They'd partied together and traveled together and had been close for many years. Krissy had gone to Marnie and Mark's wedding and had been at the hospital hours after their twins had been born, so to suddenly be privy to the horrific details surrounding the demise of their marriage? While she knew that she was going through something equally as terrible, herself, it was still devastating for Krissy to have to hear.

"The last time he put me in the hospital, I decided enough was enough," Marnie shrugged her shoulders, ready to continue explaining even as Lenore was cutting her off. She'd been trying to wedge her way into their conversation for at least a half an hour at that point, but Marnie had simply talked over her and Krissy had ended up doing the same.

"No, *I* decided that enough was enough!" Lenore finally shouted over both of them. "*I* was the one at the hospital, holding your hand when the domestic violence counselor came in and talked to you about pressing charges on him! *I* was the one who told you that enough was enough! *Me!*"

Marnie didn't seem at all phased by Lenore's outburst. She simply tipped her coffee cup back to finish the last drops and then responded as calmly as could be, while getting up to rinse it and place it in the sink. "That's true, Lenore. You stood right by my side through that whole ordeal. I couldn't have done it without you."

Lenore sat very quietly then, her back to Marnie who was still standing by the sink. She looked strangely satisfied. Krissy couldn't figure out what was going on between the two of them, but at that point she really didn't care, either. It was clear that Marnie and her mother were close, bonded in a way that was odd and unfamiliar. Yet Marnie also seemed to be able to control Lenore, to get ahold of her in a way that Krissy had never known anyone else to be able to do.

Marnie patted Lenore's shoulder and said she was going home to get the boys and would be back later with pizza and wings for dinner. Lenore agreed. Marnie hugged Krissy goodbye and Lenore retreated to her bedroom without much more than a, "I'm going to lay down," before shutting the door silently behind her. Krissy heard her TV come on a moment later.

Soon the kids and Spence were bounding back up the stairs and slamming into the kitchen. Both girls were all sticky hands and ketchup faces, and Krissy managed to wipe them clean before Spence steered them into the front bedroom where his sons stayed when they visited. The room was full of toys and stuffed animals and had a small TV, as well. He asked how the visit with Marnie had gone and Krissy said fine, though what she wanted to say was that it was weird and uncomfortable. She wanted to tell Spence that Lenore had deliberately tried to make her feel like an intruder in his apartment, a space which was supposed to be her temporary safe haven. She wanted to cry.

Spence must have sensed her frustration and sadness, because he put his arms around her and hugged her tightly. That time she didn't pull away. She wrapped her arms around her little brother's waist and hugged him back.

"Not much has changed, has it Kris?" he spoke low and close to her ear. "I keep her around to help with the boys; they love her and this divorce stuff is really hard on them. Having her here eases that for them. But she hasn't changed a bit, Kris; make no mistake about it."

Krissy leaned further into Spence and sighed. But she couldn't cry. She was too worried to cry.

Linda Dynel

Chapter 24

Shortly after Grace was born, Dorian took a new job with a bit of a salary increase and decided that they needed a bigger place. They moved into a two-bedroom apartment in a four unit building at the other end of town. The space was freshly painted and had new carpeting and Krissy wondered if a new job and a new place might provide a new perspective for Dorian. He seemed to like this newest job; he was working with kids again at a school for emotionally disturbed and behaviorally challenged children.

One of the downsides of this new job was that he was required to use physical force in order to restrain unruly, dangerous or threatening students. Soon he was practicing the holds on Krissy, using the excuse that he wanted to figure out how to administer them correctly without hurting the kids and potentially losing his job. It wasn't long before throwing her on the floor and pinning her arms behind her back, his knee in between her shoulder blades, became a matter of course in their daily life.

Once again Krissy took the brunt of Dorian's stress and frustration over having to assimilate himself to a new environment and learn the social and professional rules of yet another new employer. Dorian didn't like to have to try and fit in. He lacked proper social skills and more often than not, quickly alienated most of his co-workers by saying the wrong thing or saying the right thing but at the wrong time.

There were also more neighbors to annoy at this four-unit apartment building when Dorian and Krissy got into shouting matches. The family from the old house that lived downstairs had moved before Anna was born, and the single guy who bought the place after that couldn't have cared less if the two of them sounded like they were killing each other; he just went on smoking his weed and playing his music and nodding his head in acknowledgement when they passed him in the front foyer. Once they moved to the apartment building, though, the landlord had to call them on more than one occasion and ask them to please keep it down, as they were disturbing the other tenants. The embarrassment over this was part of the reason that Krissy quieted down and stopped fighting back. The other reason was for the sake of the girls. She hated it when he had her pinned on the floor or backed into a corner and the girls saw it. Grace would cling to Anna and the two would stand there crying, "Let Mama up, Daddy! Let Mama go! Please, Daddy!"

"No," Dorian would inevitably reply. "I'm teaching your mama a lesson. God the Father gave me to your mama to make sure that she gets into Heaven, and the only way for Mama to make it into Heaven is for her to learn to be good. You want your mama to go to Heaven, don't you, girls? Well, then, Mama needs to learn to be good and to obey Daddy!"

Two or three instances like that in the new apartment, trying to look up from where Dorian had her face mashed into the linoleum of the kitchen floor (he always tried to avoid marking the carpets with blood; he didn't want a cleaning fee coming out of their security deposit if they ended up needing to move again) or around his massive bulk as he twisted her arms in order to keep her still, watching the fear dance in her daughters eyes like tiny licks of flames, was all Krissy needed to decide that she was going to be as quiet as a church mouse no matter what Dorian did to her. Pretty soon the neighbors stopped complaining and the girls would continue to play undisturbed in their room, unaware that Daddy was taking his daily pound of flesh from their mama only a dozen or so feet away.

Krissy started working at Alfie Toaster's shortly after they moved as a way to earn a little extra money for their ever-increasing expenses. As was always the case, Dorian didn't want her leaving the house unless it was absolutely necessary, but unwilling as he was to take a second job himself, he had no choice but to encourage her to go out and get one. He swore that it was only temporary, but once her paychecks started rolling in, Dorian decided to modify his original position that women with children shouldn't work outside of the home and allowed Krissy to keep her job as an evening shift manager.

Their days were spent entirely apart now, with Fridays being the days that Dorian allowed Krissy to drive him to work so that she could have the car for grocery shopping and to run errands. She would pick up her paycheck, cash it and do whatever shopping needed to be done for the week. Since they no longer qualified for food stamps, it was a joy for Krissy to go food shopping, even though Dorian didn't allow her much to spend.

Dorian always set the trip odometer to zero before he got out of the car on Friday mornings. Krissy knew that he was well aware of what she needed to do that day and where she would be going to get it done. He didn't like her going more than five miles from the apartment, presumably because he didn't want her accidentally seeing old friends and family. He didn't want their solid, contained little family life to be disturbed.

Oddly, even staying within five miles of home didn't preclude Krissy from seeing family members, hers or his. Once when she was at the pharmacy, she saw her mother standing in line at the customer service desk. She saw the look on her mother's face and realized that Lenore had seen her, too, but when Lenore didn't make a move in her direction, Krissy simply kept right on walking out into the parking lot and went home. She thought there was very little sense in trying to say hello to her mother when Lenore clearly wasn't interested in making a move toward her. And besides, she reasoned, what good would it do to try and reconnect with any of her family members? Dorian would never allow them in her life. It was better to let sleeping dogs lie.

Then there was the time that she was standing in the grocery store checkout line. She had Grace in the child seat of the shopping cart but Anna was home with Dorian, sick with a cold. It was out of the corner of her eye that she saw the old man get in line behind her. It only took a moment to realize that the olive-skinned, gray-haired gentleman was Dorian's father. She'd only met him a couple of times, early on in her relationship with Dorian, and she was sure that he had no idea who she was. It became even more apparent that she was nothing more than a stranger to him when he spoke up, commenting to Krissy on what a beautiful little girl she had. "One of my granddaughters is about her age! What a beautiful little girl! What's her name, honey?"

Krissy was astounded. He really had no idea. "This is Grace, Dorian. She *is* your granddaughter." With that Krissy paid the cashier and left.

Dorian Sr. stood there with his mouth agape and tears rolling down his cheeks while Krissy hightailed it for the parking lot. Her mouth was dry and her heart was racing. If Dorian found out that she'd so much as made eye contact with his father, a man he claimed to despise more than anyone who'd ever lived, let alone come right out in public and told Dorian Sr. that he was looking at his own granddaughter? Well, Krissy thought, she might very well end up in a world of hurt more severe than she'd ever experienced before.

With a little more money came a little more freedom of movement for their family, but Dorian decided how and when that money would be spent, even down to the last entertainment dollar. No matter where he decided to take his family, whether it was to the local waterpark or to dinner or very rarely to a movie, he always made sure that they stopped at church first in order to pray. There would be no fun before prayers. There would also be no fun if at any point during any activity, Dorian felt as though Krissy had embarrassed him or believed that someone was looking at him or his family with disdain. Dorian would pick up and leave whole meals at restaurants if he imagined that the waiter might have spit in their food. He would abandon movies if he heard people whispering behind them, always assuming that they were whispering about him or Krissy or the girls. He once left Krissy and the girls in the parking lot of an amusement park and drove away, after storming out of the park gates because he believed that Krissy had deliberately tried to embarrass him. He'd left them for over an hour while he sat in an out of the way area and watched her sit and cry and then rally the girls and quietly decide what to do. He explained that he was trying to teach her a lesson when he finally drove back around in order to pick them up and go home.

Not a day went by that Dorian didn't inflict mental and emotional torture on Krissy. It became part of their routine, part of the culture of their household. Dorian could rant for hours; mean, filthy words spilling from his mouth. Krissy learned to act as though she were tuning him out, though she always heard every word. The physical toll was just as bad. It was a day-to-day decision on what she could wear; long sleeves, three quarter sleeves or short sleeves? And shorts in the summertime? Almost never, but she became an expert at adapting and always had an excuse for cashiers and co-workers alike as to why it was that she dressed so oddly in the warmer months.

The summer of 1999 was the worst of her entire adult life. She dreaded everything about her time with Dorian, especially the nighttime. She started sleeping in a recliner in order to avoid having to sleep next to him, though she told Dorian that it made her legs feel better when they were raised, after standing at the restaurant for eight hours. The truth was that his touch made her skin crawl and she couldn't maintain sleep when she was constantly worried about waking up with him on top of her. Though Dorian had never been one to drink, he told Krissy to start buying wine while she was out on her Friday shopping trips. He said that he needed to unwind after work, but pretty soon he was drinking the cheap red wine directly from the glass gallon jug as soon as he walked in the door every afternoon. Though Krissy couldn't have cared less if he drank himself into a stupor every day for the rest of his life, she worried that he might continue drinking after she'd left for work and that something bad might happen to the girls as a result.

When he wasn't deliberately making her life miserable, Dorian was obsessing over the New Millennium. He was convinced that the Apocalypse was coming and that 144,000 good, forthright Roman Catholics would be taken directly into Heaven to live with God the Father forever in Eternal Bliss. He believed the remainder of the Roman Catholics - those of lesser virtue - would be left behind. In order to prove to God the Father that he and his family were worthy to be taken directly into Heaven, Dorian hung a shelf high above their couch and installed a crucifix over it. He kept a candle burning on it at all times and called it their Family Altar. He said special prayers before work every day and increased the amount of charitable donations he was sending overseas to Catholic relief organizations. He explained to Krissy that the End of the World was coming. He told her that she needed to believe that, and that she needed to pray for their family just as he was doing. He told her that if she didn't, she would surely burn in the Eternal Fires of Hell while he and the girls went on to Eternal Bliss in Heaven, where they would live with the Holy Trinity and the Blessed Mother and all of the angels and saints for all time and eternity.

While Dorian prayed every day that he and his wife and children might have clean enough souls to be four of the 144,000 taken directly into Heaven during the Apocalypse, he also prepared for every contingency. He started buying weaponry, which he called his End of the World Arsenal. He told Krissy that he wanted to be prepared for anything.

Krissy continued to pray and work and shop and live within the four walls and five miles that she was allowed. She didn't know if Dorian was right or not; she had to admit that she was not as well versed in the Bible as he was, nor did she watch all of the religious programming that he watched on the new television that he'd recently purchased. She didn't listen to the multiple religious radio programs that he still listened to on his shortwave radio. She had no idea whether the world was going to end in four months or not. All she really knew was that she'd promised to be married to Dorian forever, but that forever was beginning to seem like a mighty long time. In fact, forever was beginning to seem impossible.

There were times when all she could think about was how much she wished she could simply die. She wanted to escape but didn't know how. How could she leave the man who was the head of her household? The man whom she believed that God had put in her life for a reason. The father of her children. The man she had promised to love and cherish and obey for the rest of her life. How could she break that promise to God?

But then there was the matter of the girls. Was it even healthy for them to be living in that tiny apartment day in and day out with no friends and no family, without there even being the hope of public or parochial school as a distraction and a light; an opening to the outside world? What if something happened to her? They would be left with Dorian alone to care for them. No, killing herself wouldn't solve anything, she decided. That's when she started thinking that maybe she wasn't the one who needed to go.

There was a drain in the floor of the basement that had recently backed up and had flooded raw sewage all around their storage area and brand-new washer and dryer. It had been disgusting and smelly and Krissy had refused to go into the basement until the landlord had gotten the pipe repaired and a crew had come to clean up the mess. Not long after that, Krissy saw a TV show about a girl who suffered from Munchausen Syndrome. The narrator explained that the girl had been ingesting her own feces in order to keep herself sick, and how that behavior had almost killed her.

For weeks after she'd seen the show, every time Krissy went into the basement to do laundry, she would glance at the drain in the floor. She wondered just how much raw sewage someone would need to ingest in order to do more than simply send them to the hospital with a severe stomach ache. She also wondered how a person wouldn't notice that they were actually ingesting the foul-smelling stuff. Not being sure of the answers to either question, Krissy stopped pondering the drain and simply let the idea pass.

She worked New Years Eve of 1999. Another shift manager, Kim, had worked with her that night. After they'd finished their closing duties, the two women opened a small bottle of champagne that Kim had brought in order to toast the New Millennium. Krissy knew that Kim was in an unhappy marriage, too, so she felt comfortable confiding in her about some of her troubles at home, though she never, ever, went into detail about the abuse that Dorian inflicted upon her. As far Kim knew, Krissy was simply married to a big, uncaring jerk, same as she was. When they toasted around ten-thirty and Kim jokingly wished speedy and tidy divorces for both of them in the New Year, Krissy almost choked on her champagne.

Divorce? It wasn't a possibility. Not an option. Not in her religion, anyway. But as soon as Kim had spoken the word a sharp feeling, much like a lightning bolt, went racing through Krissy's body.

Leaving Dorian

Divorce.

She went home that night and laid down under her pile of blankets on their old couch. Dorian sat in the recliner and waited, rosary in hand, while he watched Dick Clark count down to the New Millennium. Krissy's eyes started to close around a quarter to twelve. She heard Dorian turn off the TV sometime later and then noted the lights in the kitchen being turned off, though her eyes were closed. She covered her head with the blankets once she heard Dorian close his bedroom door and she smiled. It was 2000, and they were all still there.

Dorian was meaner than usual the first two weeks of January, and Krissy knew why, but after the shame of being so completely wrong wore off, he went back to his usual level of nastiness and their little family relaxed back into life as usual. Or so Dorian thought. After Kim's New Year's toast, divorce was literally all Krissy could think about almost every waking moment.

She decided that somewhere inside of her angry, mean, and most likely mentally-ill husband there had to be a part of him that was calm. Reasonable. Sane. Around Valentine's Day Krissy decided that the best thing to do would be to sit Dorian down and simply talk to him about their situation. It was obvious that he didn't love her, and though she faked love for him, she figured that he had to know how she really felt. So, one afternoon before work she asked him to sit with her in the living room while the girls played in their bedroom and tried to have a heart-to-heart talk. She explained that she knew how stressful it was for him to have to be married to her; that she knew that he didn't love her but that she didn't love him anymore either, and that it would probably be better for everyone concerned if the two of them just called it quits; shared the girls and simply moved on with their individual lives. They could look into the annulment process; there was always a chance that the Church might find grounds on which to nullify their union. If that happened, they would both be free to move on; maybe even to marry again, someday.

Dorian sat very still for a moment. It was a beautiful winter day and the sunbeams shone brightly through the venetian blinds that hung on their living room windows. He was sitting just on the edge of the recliner where Krissy usually slept. His hands were folded and his elbows were resting on his knees. He was rubbing his lower lip with one index finger. Then he stopped. He looked Krissy square in the eye and said, "I will never let you go. If you ever try and leave me, I will kill you, and then I'll kill the girls. Do you understand?" His voice wasn't raised; it was flat and even and his facial expression was as calm as if he were talking about what they were going to have for dinner that evening.

"But Dorian," Krissy protested, not sure if she should continue to force the point. Considering how calm he seemed, she thought that it was at least worth a shot. He couldn't seriously be threatening to kill her. He was just trying to scare her. Surely, he was only trying to scare her. "We don't love each other. This whole thing, this marriage, it's no good for the girls. They shouldn't see what goes on between us. They shouldn't ..."

Dorian interrupted her. He'd laced his fingers tightly together and his jaw was suddenly squared. His voice was raised now and his tone was sharp and deliberate. "I'm going to tell you this once and once only. If you ever try and leave me, I'll kill you. I'll snap your neck like a twig. You'll be dead before your body hits the ground. And then I'll kill the girls. I won't have them living in this world without me. Do you understand, you ungrateful whore? Your family will never, ever, get a hold of my precious daughters. They're *mine*."

Krissy was in shock. She realized all at once that Dorian was completely serious and that even bringing up the topic could have resulted in him reaching over at that very moment and strangling the life out of her, just like he'd nearly done in their kitchen almost five years before. She was so scared she could barely squeak out a feeble and breathless, "Yes".

"Then we're done here," he said, getting up and walking into the kitchen.

Krissy sat there for another moment before she regained enough strength in her legs to silently tiptoe past where he stood in the kitchen, getting a snack. She crept into the girls' room and laid down on Anna's bed and tried not to cry.

Dear God, she prayed silently, please help me.

Leaving Dorian

Linda Dynel

Chapter 25

Krissy unpacked as best she could in the cramped back bedroom while Spence worked at his computer and the girls watched TV and played with their cousin's toys. At five minutes after four she sat on the edge of Spence's bed and folded her hands. She prayed an Our Father, a Hail Mary, and a Glory Be. She prayed that when Dorian walked out into the parking lot and discovered that the car was gone, he would simply walk the four blocks and catch the bus home, not call the police and report the car missing. If he took the bus home, he would be walking in the door at around four-forty. He'd storm into the house mad as hell and ready to take a bite out of Krissy. But then she and the girls wouldn't be there and he would see the note that she'd left on the counter. If he called the police instead of taking the bus, there was no telling what would happen next. Would they find the car, all the way out where she was? Did police agencies in the area share information like that, and would they even care to, considering how old the car was? Krissy swallowed the lump of fear and dread that made her feel as though she were choking. She took a deep breath in, held it, then tried to exhale slowly. Her hands were shaking and she wanted to cry but she didn't. She listened closely for police sirens.

Please, God, she prayed silently, please don't let him find me.

Around five-thirty Marnie arrived again, this time with food, and her sons trailing behind her. The last time Krissy had seen them they were barely two years old; still pudgy, sandy-haired bundles of energy. Now they were two dark-haired preteens with sullen expressions and hands jammed into their pants pockets, their identical faces sporting identical hints of moustaches to come.

She'd anticipated wanting to hug them, wrapping her arms around them and cuddling them like she had when they were babies, but they were not the children that she'd walked away from almost a decade before. They were strangers. They said the briefest of hellos, trying hard not to make eye contact with the unfamiliar lady, then hugged Lenore with not much more enthusiasm. Once they'd filled paper plates with pizza and wings, they headed off into the living room with a game they'd brought to use in Spence's PlayStation.

Marnie apologized for the twins but Krissy brushed it off. "They don't know me, Marn. It's fine."

The girls came in from the front bedroom and Krissy washed their hands and set them up in chairs around the table. She cut their pizza and picked chicken off the bones for them. Marnie filled small plastic tumblers with soda and when Krissy suggested milk, Marnie smiled and suggested that Krissy lighten up. Krissy bit her tongue and allowed the soda to be put in front of the girls. Walking away from Dorian meant giving up some of the control she'd had over her girls; she understood that very clearly now. People and places and things in the world - heck, even her own family - would immediately change things for the girls, big things and small things alike. There was no more cocoon; no more safe haven. She had taken her daughters and exposed them to uncertainty. Whatever happened from that point on, good or bad, was on her and she knew that Dorian would never let her forget that.

Krissy stood against the dishwasher while Lenore and Marnie sat chatting and eating at the kitchen table with the girls. Her stomach was in knots. The clock said five-forty-five. Even if Dorian had called the police from work, he would definitely be home by then. He would have seen the note and realized that all of the girls' clothes and some of their toys and Krissy's things were gone and he would be doing ... what? Krissy had no idea. Raging? Slamming and storming around the apartment? Praying? Devising a plan of action to find and rescue his daughters from the clutches of his mentally diseased and wretchedly sinful wife? Krissy tried to figure out who he'd call to help him find her. The police, for sure, but she didn't think they could do anything, anyway. He had her note explaining why she'd left and that her lawyer would be contacting him. Legally, she knew she was in the right. And as far as Dorian finding her? Well, he wasn't omniscient, she reminded herself.

"Kris, why don't you sit down and eat?" Marnie suggested.

"I can't; I'm too nervous. I'm..." Krissy started, and then it occurred to her; the weapons were still in the car. If he did find her, somehow, she was sure he'd try and take the car back.

"What's wrong?" Lenore asked. Krissy looked as though she'd seen a ghost.

"Let's get you guys cleaned up," Krissy suggested as she cleared Anna and Grace's plates and cups and washed their hands and faces at the sink. Then she scooted them back into the front bedroom and sat down at the table with Marnie. "The stuff. It's still in the trunk."

Marnie put down her soda and wiped her fingers with a second paper napkin. She thought a minute, then looked at Lenore, who seemed surprisingly clear, calm and focused again. "You've got to turn them in," Lenore said. "Call the police and explain what's going on and ask that they take them and destroy them. You can't have them anywhere near you, honey. And especially not in the car. If you get pulled over and the police find that stuff in your car, you'll be the one getting hauled off to jail."

"I agree," Marnie said, standing up and tossing her paper plate into the trash, "but first I think it's time we call your old man. At least then you can tell the cops what kind of a mood he's in and whether he's home or not and maybe out looking for you. You can also give them your old address so that they can contact the police out there to keep an eye on him."

"Yes, but you can't have her call from here. Take her to the pay phone around the corner by the car wash and have her call from there." Lenore was strangely efficient in her thoughts, now, acting adult and capable and lucid. Krissy was feeling more and more like she was hearing everyone talking around her from somewhere deep inside of a big, plastic bubble.

"I've got the kids," Lenore said to Marnie quietly, leaning around Krissy to peek in on the girls. "Just take her and try and call him. Have her tell him she's not coming home; just what we talked about. Then get her right back here. And be careful. You have no idea if he's out there. I mean, the chances are slim to none that he could have found her this quickly, but ..."

"What's going on?" Spence was suddenly standing in the kitchen archway. He looked angry or worried or some other unpleasant emotion that Krissy couldn't quite put her finger on. She felt Marnie pushing her green fleece sweatshirt against her hand.

"I'm taking Kris to call Dorian, just to see what frame of mind he's in and to make sure that he's at home and not out looking for her yet. She's still got to turn the weapons in to the police, too, so she's got to figure out ..."

"Whoa, whoa, whoa! Do you really think it's a good idea that you take her outta here in the near dark? Can't this wait 'til tomorrow?"

Spence's voice was raising in volume and pitch but it seemed to be getting further away and Krissy felt more and more like she was falling backwards, down, down, down the rabbit hole. The three of them were talking about her like she wasn't even in the room, and Krissy was letting them, though she couldn't figure out why. Then Grace was standing at her side, tugging on the hand that held her green fleece sweatshirt. She had her own tiny jacket in her hands. "We go home, Mama?"

All at once the air left Krissy lungs and she started to cry. Huge, fat tears rolled down her cheeks and she simply stood there, shaking. She couldn't make her hands reach out for her daughter. She was suddenly terrified and confused. She didn't want to have to talk to Dorian. She didn't want to have to hear his voice, to hear him yelling and calling her filthy names. And she had no idea what she was going to say to him. How in the world was she going to tell Dorian that she wasn't coming home?

Spence picked Grace up and kissed her cheek, gently removing the jacket from her grasp. "Come here, sweetie," he said, his voice so reassuring that it made Krissy cry even harder. "Don't you remember what we talked about? You guys are gonna stay her with me and Grandma for a little while. Doesn't that sound like a good plan?" he asked, smiling broadly and pulling a big bag of licorice from a cabinet. Grace smiled and reached for the candy and the two disappeared into the living room.

Krissy felt Marnie's hand on her back. "Come on, girl," she said as she pushed Krissy toward the door. "Let's get this over with."

Linda Dynel

Chapter 26

It was by a stroke of luck that Krissy had seen Spencer at all. She hadn't been scheduled to work that day, but a server had called in sick and knowing that Krissy was always looking to make a little extra money, her manager always called her first to cover available dining room shifts.

Krissy saw them as she was punching in. Breathless with surprise and anticipation, she'd hurriedly stored her purse in the back office. Then she stood at the waitress station and just looked at them; Spence and his little family. His wife Chloe was bigger than Krissy remembered, but after two kids, who wasn't? Their older boy who looked to be maybe five years old was coloring a placemat while their towheaded toddler sat with his back to her in one of the restaurant's bulky wooden highchairs at the end of the booth. Gazing intently at the two children, Krissy realized that those weren't just Spencer's little boys, they were her nephews, as well. And though Spence and Chloe didn't speak a word to each other, and their entire body posture spoke volumes about their unhappiness and the stress that their family must have been under, Krissy couldn't help but take those few steps across the tiled floor and onto the blue and green striped carpet of the dining room. She stood at the end of their table just behind the highchair for the briefest of moments just drinking them in, these strangers who were actually her family. Spence looked up, thinking it was his server. Then he looked again.

"Oh my God ..." he stuttered, standing up quickly and bumping his thigh into the side of the table. "Oh my God! I didn't know you worked here!" He grabbed Krissy and hugged her, then pulled her back, looked at her and hugged her again.

Krissy tried not to recoil. She wanted to hug him back so badly but knew that there was no point. She could never have him back in her life. The shame of it, of rejecting her own brother in favor of anyone or anything else, stung her heart. Her throat felt tight and she tried not to cry. She tried especially hard not to look at his sons, though they were both looking intently up at her. Chloe, on the other hand, sat tight lipped and unsmiling, her face a mask of dread and apprehension.

"Holy shit, Kris! How long *have* you worked here?" Spence was getting loud with excitement and Chloe was looking like she wanted to crawl under the table, her round cheeks glowing pink with embarrassment.

"Oh, a couple of years. How are you guys?" Krissy smiled at the boys while avoiding eye contact with Chloe. The two women had never really gotten along, for reasons that were never entirely clear to Krissy. But by the look on Chloe's face, though, Krissy could tell that it was still crystal clear to her why the two had never gotten along, and even after so many years apart it seemed that Chloe still had no desire to mend any fences with her sister-in-law.

The older boy looked at his mother and then at Krissy. He didn't smile, taking the very clear yet unspoken cue that the lady chatting with his dad was not someone he needed to be nice to. It seemed as though Spence was starting to feel the tension, as well. "We're good, really good," he lied, chancing just the briefest glance at his clearly embarrassed wife. "This is Ethan," he said, ruffling the older boy's hair, "and this little monster is baby Jared!"

"Oh, my goodness, they're beautiful!" Krissy gushed. She tried to think of something to say to Chloe to try and smooth things over, because she could see by the look on her sister-in-law's face that Spence was gonna catch hell when she finally got him out of that restaurant. People don't change, Krissy reminded herself.

"I saw your wedding video!" Krissy suddenly remembered, turning to face Chloe. "Grandma Patty and Grandpa Sam brought me a VHS copy years ago one of the times that I saw them for lunch. Your dress was beautiful, and what an interesting venue! I had no idea before I saw it that you could get married at the zoo!" It was the only thing Krissy could think to say, under the circumstances; the details of their wedding day were one of the very few things she knew about her brother and sister-in-law's life together.

Chloe just nodded her head and smiled tightly, forcing an almost inaudible 'thanks' before Spence spoke up and ended the conversation. "Well, it was great to see you, Kris; really great! Um…" Both boys were getting antsy and though she wanted nothing more than to keep standing there with her brother, she could see that Chloe was probably mere seconds away from gathering up her children and walking out. Having to witness Spence's reaction to seeing his sister again after so many years apart was becoming too much for her, and Krissy didn't know how much more Chloe was going to be able to take.

Since no one knew better than Krissy what it was like to dread going home because you knew you were going to be walking straight into a shit storm, your spouse having transformed into a raving lunatic because something out of the ordinary happened or something didn't go their way, she decided right then and there that she would walk away from her brother again, for his sake as well as for her own. She knew that they could never be a real family; Dorian would never allow it. There was no point in continuing to stand there pining for something that could never be.

"It was great to see you. All of you," Krissy said, smiling at Ethan who was playing with his straw while Jared was trying mightily to free himself from the strap that secured him to his highchair. She gave Spence one last hug and walked away and into the back room, where she sat down at the manager's desk and cried.

Cooks and severs alike came back and asked what was wrong, but Krissy just said that she was having an off day and that she'd be fine. She couldn't imagine how she'd try and explain to anyone why she was crying. To say out loud that she couldn't reconnect with a brother whom she hadn't seen in years because of what her husband might do to her if he somehow found out? No way. She knew how wrong her life was, but she certainly didn't want anyone else to know; especially not her co-workers. They respected her, and she wasn't prepared to lose that respect by admitting that she was married to a man who beat her, emotionally and physically, every day. Krissy dried her tears and started waiting tables, only glancing at Spence and his family now and then when she thought she could manage to do it without drawing attention to herself.

Less than an hour later Spence and his family got up to leave. He left a tip on the table before heading toward the men's room while Chloe walked the boys past Krissy, who was punching in an order at the server's station. She didn't acknowledge Krissy and Krissy was not surprised. She held Ethan by the hand and Jared in her arms and kept her eyes fixed forward. Neither boy looked at Krissy. She fully expected Spence to do the same and half turned away when she saw him walking toward her, but then he stopped and she knew she had to face him. He was holding something out to her. "If you ever need me," Spence almost whispered, pressing his business card into her cold hand, "just call."

"I don't know how Chloe would feel about that..."

The words were barely out of her mouth before Spence spoke again, shaking his head and biting his lip like he was trying to hold something back. "Don't worry about her, Kris. I'm telling you, if you ever need anything, you call me, O.K? Promise?"

She slipped the business card into the front pocket of her apron with her tips. She didn't know what to think or what to say but she hugged her brother goodbye and said she loved him and promised just the same. One thing was for sure; she knew that she couldn't keep that business card. She watched him walk out the door and wished with her whole heart that she was walking out with him.

Linda Dynel

Chapter 27

Krissy put on her jacket as she walked down the stairs behind Marnie. She could feel the soft bulk of the fleece against her skin, but her arms didn't feel like her own; they felt heavy and dull. When they got to the bottom of the stairs, Marnie told Krissy to stand back in the shadows while she walked into the mudroom to check things out. Then she poked her head out of the screen door and took a long look around. "I think we're good," she said as she took a step back in. "Come on."

Krissy wanted to throw up. Fear crawled up the back of her neck and over her scalp. What if he was waiting just around the corner? Marnie's SUV was parked almost at the end of the short block. What if when she was walking up to the passenger door he came out of nowhere and attacked her? Marnie was tiny; there was no way she would be able to defend her against Dorian.

Krissy walked toward the SUV, though it felt as though she was floating. She reached for the door handle but the door seemed to swing open on its own. Marnie was already behind the wheel. "Come on, Kris. We gotta go do this. Now."

Krissy pulled herself up onto the passenger seat. She could feel the cool of the upholstery through her jeans. The truck smelled like cigarette smoke and perfume. She loved the smell of stale cigarette smoke; it always reminded her of Buzby.

Marnie jammed the SUV into reverse and Krissy fastened her seat belt. She didn't know how far Marnie was taking her, but then they were at a payphone and Marnie was pushing quarters into her hand and telling her what to say; that she and the girls were safe and that she wasn't coming home. That she was filing for divorce. Short and sweet. No chitter-chatter. No yelling or fighting or crying. In and out. Over and done. "Got it, Kris?"

Krissy nodded her head but wasn't really sure what the hell was going on. She felt light headed and scared and hollow. Marnie had told her to leave the car door open, so she did. She picked up the cold receiver. She could feel the gravel under her feet. Eighteen-wheelers sped by and Krissy wondered where she was. Somewhere in Hamburg. What road was her brother's house on again? Where exactly were her daughters?

Suddenly, she couldn't remember any of the details of her new life. If Marnie were to drive away right then, drive away and leave her standing there all alone, would she even be able to find her way back to Anna and Grace? Krissy felt an overwhelming sense of being lost and alone. A tiny speck in a big world. She dialed her home phone number and waited. One ring. Two rings. And then, "Kris?" Dorian was breathless. His voice was small and scared and desperate. "Krissy?? Is that you???"

"Yes," She wasn't sure if she'd actually spoken; the fear gripping her throat was tighter than his hands had ever been around her neck.

"Oh my God, Krissy, where are you? Oh my God ... bring the girls home to me, please!! I swear to you, Kris, I'll never hurt you again! I swear! And you can have your family back! I swear on my life, Kris, everything will change! Everything! I'll ..."

She was studying the distorted reflection of herself in the telephone's shiny keypad while she tried to remember what it was that Marnie had told her to say. Dorian didn't sound like himself and she thought that was a very good thing. It made it easier to recite the words she'd been given as she remembered them. "I'm fine and the girls are fine and I'm filing for divorce. There's gonna be a rest ..." How she was speaking the words? She had no idea. It was still impossibly difficult to stand up to him, even though he was groveling and crying and begging and pleading. It felt wrong, so very wrong, to challenge Dorian; so very wrong to tell Dorian what was going to happen instead of acquiescing to his rants and demands. "... a restraining order put into place. Um .... you won't be able to come within one hundred yards..."

"No, Krissy; *no!*" Dorian bellowed, crying and sobbing into the phone. "Oh my God, Kris, please, *please* bring the girls home to me! I'll do whatever you want, I promise! We'll go to church less! No more hours of praying, O.K? And I'll let you see your family whenever you want! Kris, please, *please*, don't do this to me! Don't do this to our family! Come home, Krissy! Please come home!"

She kept on, but it was getting harder to listen to Dorian cry. He was in so much pain. She could hear the anguish in his voice and what seemed like true and sincere sorrow. It ripped at her heart. He seemed sad, so sad, and it was her fault. "Um ... one hundred yards, or ... or ..." Krissy took a deep breath, then exhaled the words, "...or you'll be arrested." She hadn't expected that he'd be crying. She'd expected him to be yelling and ranting and threatening her.

"Arrested?" Dorian howled like a wounded animal. "*Arrested?* Dear God, Krissy, please! No! You've gotta come home Kris! You've gotta come home right now!"

Krissy was shuffling her feet in the gravel anxiously. She looked up at the darkening sky and tried to decide what she should do.

"Krissy! *Kris!*" Marnie was trying to get her attention, whispering sharply from the dark interior of the SUV.

Krissy looked over at her, perplexed. She couldn't ever remember feeling so exhausted and confused. "He said I have to come home. He wants me to come home now."

Marnie's expression changed from annoyance to one of fear and panic. "Hang up the phone!" she shouted, popping the SUV into reverse and backing up, then pulling forward again so that the open passenger door was almost touching Krissy's arm. "Hang up that fucking phone and get your ass in here now! *Now!*"

Krissy was surprised and shocked that Marnie was suddenly yelling at her and though she could still hear Dorian wailing through the receiver, she did what she was told and hung up the phone. Then she pulled herself into the passenger's seat.

Leaving Dorian

Marnie crawled over her and slammed the door closed behind her. "Jesus, Kris!" Marnie was laughing now, but Krissy knew that it was only nervous laughter. "You scared the shit out of me! Fuck!"

Krissy sat silent and still as Marnie drove across the street and into the parking lot of a gas station convenience store. "I gotta get a beer. You want anything?"

Krissy shook her head no.

"You don't drink anymore?"

"I haven't," Krissy whispered.

Marnie laughed a nervous laugh again and then sighed. She looked at her friend with a mix of pity and love. "Look, Kris, I know everything is all fucked up right now. And I know how hard that was for you, to have to listen to him crying and pleading like that. I went through the same shit with Mark. But believe me, Kris, if you go back to him, it'll be the same old bullshit times a hundred, if you ever even make it out the front door alive again. This is your one shot, Kris. No going back." Marnie tried to catch Krissy's gaze; she seemed to be staring past her and out into the night. "O.K, Kris?"

Krissy nodded. She didn't want to go back to Dorian, ever. She just had no idea how she was going to live without him.

Chapter 28

It was the first week of April and the weather was warming up. Dorian insisted that the windows remain closed until it was truly warm, ever afraid that something like opening the windows and letting the heat out would anger the landlord and get them evicted. But it was such a beautiful, warm spring day that Krissy had cracked open both living room windows and the dining room window in order to allow a shallow cross breeze in to freshen things up. She had been gathering laundry and was walking down their short hallway to the living room when out of nowhere she heard a voice. It was low and small but also strong and deep. And familiar.

"I do not want you living like this."

The message literally stopped her in her tracks. A chill ran up her spine. She stood there a moment, hands tightly gripping the laundry basket she'd filled in the girls' room only moments before.

She'd been praying for help for years, praying for some clear-cut directive so that she might understand how to fix what was clearly broken in their lives. She had also taken to praying for healing for Dorian; praying that he might somehow be made whole. Better. If only Dorian could be healed, then maybe her marriage could be healed, too. But now there was this voice. Here. With her. And it wasn't talking about Dorian or her marriage or the girls. It was talking about *her*.

Krissy walked down into the basement and loaded the washing machine. It was always quiet and dim and cool in the basement, and she enjoyed going down there even just for a few minutes every day. But now she felt uncomfortable. She stood in front of their storage space and stared at all of the boxes of baby clothes and stacks of baby items that she'd piled into the roomy twelve by twelve space. She'd saved all of Anna and Grace's things just in case she ever had another baby.

But she didn't want another baby. Not with Dorian. Her face started to feel hot and her palms had started to sweat and all at once she wanted to cry. She wanted out. Now. She wanted to run upstairs and grab the girls and run away. It was the most overwhelming urge she'd ever felt to do anything, other than the urge to be a mother. She did not want to be married to Dorian anymore. She especially did not, under any circumstances, want to risk getting pregnant by him again. She was tired of listening to him berate and degrade her every day. She didn't want to endure one more kick to the ribs, one more slap to the back of the head, one more push to the ground while his body covered hers and his face was so close, she could smell his breath filling her nostrils and his lips were so close while he called her filthy names that he could just as easily have kissed her.

Krissy was done.

She ran upstairs and locked the front door behind her. Then she listened at the girls' door. She could hear Grace softly snoring and Anna turning the pages of a book. She tiptoed to the kitchen and grabbed the phone book out from under the sink. She looked up lawyers. *Matrimonial.* Farther down the page she found Legal Aid Services. Well, that was a stroke of luck, she thought, because they had no savings and she had no idea how much it cost to get divorced or how she was going to pay for it, anyway. Nothing seemed to make sense and she had no idea what she was actually looking at and she started to feel anxious and scared. She wanted out and she wanted out that very second. And what did you say when you called a lawyer? Did she have to talk about the abuse right there on the phone? And should she even call from their home phone? Were the calls made from their phone listed on the bill? Dorian handled all of the bills; he didn't even like her to open them, so she had no idea how the billing system worked. She sat on the edge of the bed that they were supposed to be sharing but that she only laid in when she couldn't avoid it anymore, and thought. She thought about her faith and her Church. She thought about what leaving Dorian and filing for divorce would mean for her as a Catholic woman. Then she thought about what the voice had said.

The answer was clear; it was time to go, and she was going. She just didn't know how.

That evening Krissy made an excuse to Dorian and went into work a half an hour early. She was careful not to let her body posture or her tone of voice tip Dorian off that there might be something wrong. Sometimes it felt as though he could read her thoughts. She knew in her reasonable mind that that was ridiculous; he just knew her well and could anticipate things she would say and do just like she could with him after so many years together. Still, though, she tried to clear her mind and slow her breathing and leave the house as seemingly unaffected as possible.

As soon as she got to work, she went straight into the back office and looked up Legal Aid again. It was four-thirty and she wanted to make sure that she spoke to someone before the close of business that day. Cooks came and went, punching in and rifling through stock shelves and tried to hear what it was that Krissy was talking about. She spoke in a hushed tone, though she knew that she probably didn't need to; nothing she was saying would ever get back to Dorian. No one that she worked with had ever even met him. He'd made it clear that he thought that Krissy's co-workers were beneath him in every way, and had no intention of ever meeting them.

Legal Aid explained that their services were based on need and a sliding scale fee, but that it could take up to a year or more for a divorce to go through. The lady that Krissy spoke with also recommended taking advantage of their mediation services, as opposed to using one of their lawyers. She said that in some cases, mediation was a more civil and expeditious way for a divorce to proceed.

Krissy paused, a long, thoughtful pause that made the lady on the other end of the line say, "Hello? Hello?" and ask if she was still there. Krissy took a deep breath and said that yes, she was still there but that there was something else.

She'd never before spoken the words; never told anyone what had been going on between her and Dorian. But now she would have to. Now was the time. She turned to make sure that there wasn't a cook or server standing anywhere near the office door, and then she started.

The words choked her at first and she had to clear her throat and the lady asked her to speak up. When Krissy explained that she was in a domestic violence situation and that when she'd brought up divorce to her husband on a separate occasion that he'd threatened to kill her and the kids if she ever tried to leave, the lady said that Krissy needed to contact a battered woman's shelter and get herself and her children into a safe house before any sort of legal action could begin. She sounded like she was reading from a script and Krissy started to wonder how often women called and said that they were being beaten by their husbands? So frequently that Legal Aid had prescribed talking points for their phone counselors to read? Krissy thanked the lady and hung up.

A safe house? It hadn't occurred to Krissy that she'd need to think about taking the girls to a shelter. For some reason she thought that once the divorce papers were filed that Dorian would be removed from the apartment by the police and that she would be able to continue living there with the girls. But realistically, she thought, sitting there with the phone book still open on her lap, how would that actually work? There was no way that Dorian would simply stay away, even if the police themselves removed him. He'd be back within minutes, she knew, pounding on the windows and at the front door, yelling at the top of his lungs to be let back into his own home. Dorian would never be rebuked. He would never be stopped. That was why she'd thought about killing herself, and then about killing him. She had no idea how she was ever going to actually get away from him for good.

Tears filled her eyes and she let them fall. She sat there drying her cheeks and blowing her nose when her manager Dan walked in and asked what was wrong. She decided that it was no use keeping her home life a secret anymore, especially because if she was

Linda Dynel

going to leave Dorian, then her boss would have to know eventually, anyway. She asked Dan to come out back with her and after closing the heavy security door behind them she told him the whole ugly truth. It was easier telling Dan than it had been telling the lady at Legal Aid just moments before, and though her palms were sweating and her face was red with embarrassment and shame, her guts had started to feel lighter and the knot sitting in her belly wasn't quite as tight.

When Krissy finished speaking, Dan wiped at his forehead with the back of his hand. He looked as though he'd been hit with a bucket of cold water; shocked and horrified and overwhelmed. Then he couldn't hold the tears back anymore and he cried and she cried and he told her that he'd never even suspected such things and that he was so sorry that she'd been living that way. He told her that she should do whatever she needed to and that he would work out her schedule around her situation for as long as she needed him to. He hugged her and told her that she was a good person and that she didn't deserve to be treated like that for one more day.

He asked her what she was going to do and she explained the Legal Aid dilemma and told him that she didn't want to have to live in a battered woman's shelter. Dan suggested that she try getting in touch with family members to help her out and Krissy said that she'd think about it.

The next day she went into the basement while the girls were napping and dug out an old personal phone book that she had stashed away in between some old school papers and books in the back of the storage space, behind the boxes of baby clothes. Inside was her grandparent's Florida address and phone number. Krissy couldn't imagine that they would have moved since the last time she'd spoken to them, and she thought that they might be as good a place to start as any. Maybe they could send her money, or maybe they could point her in the direction of another family member who could help.

She called them from work that night and while they were just pleased as punch to hear from her, they didn't offer to send her any money and she felt funny asking, considering she hadn't spoken to them in so long. She explained that she was going through a divorce and that she'd be sure to start calling them more frequently and that she'd even send pictures of the girls as soon as she could. When she asked for her Aunt Karen's phone number, Lenore's older sister, they were happy to give it to her and wished her well and told her to keep in touch. Krissy hung up the phone and took a deep breath.

Her Aunt Karen hadn't ever been the kind of person that you called when you needed emotional support or a kind word, but she was extremely wealthy. She lived in one of the most prestigious communities in Western New York, one with million-dollar properties and a Homeowner's Association. Krissy knew that the chance was slim to none that her aunt would offer to help her out financially, let alone house her and the girls, but she knew that she needed to exhaust every possible option. She wanted to cry. Instead, she dialed her Aunt Karen's number and prayed that she was home.

Karen's husband, Richard, answered the phone, and when he realized who it was that he was speaking to, Krissy could hear the excitement rising in his voice. He asked her to hold a moment and Krissy could hear him talking to someone in hushed tones. Then suddenly her Aunt Karen was on the line, her voice tight and controlled. Karen had never been a woman of great warmth or tenderness. She'd always been the family member that criticized when she should have tried to be understanding; shook hands and air-kissed when she should have embraced and given a pat on the back.

Krissy explained that she was getting in touch with family members again because she was divorcing Dorian. Her aunt said that she was sorry to hear that. Krissy told her that she had two daughters now and their ages, and her aunt said that she couldn't wait to meet them. The conversation slowed down almost immediately as it always tended to with her Aunt Karen, and Krissy decided all at once that if she were going to get any help from her well-to-do aunt that she was going to need to tell her exactly what was going on. She took a deep breath and explained that she was not just reaching out to reconnect after all the years away, but that she and her daughters were in danger. The three of them needed a place to stay, and as soon as possible.

There was a pause when Krissy finished speaking, a pause so long that Krissy almost thought that perhaps her aunt was trying to hold back tears. But then she spoke up and explained that under no circumstances could she have Krissy and the girls stay with her. Though her home was certainly spacious enough to accommodate the three of them, what if Dorian found them? Her address and phone number were listed in the phone book. What if he made a scene in front of her neighbors? Good Lord, what would the neighbors think?? No, Karen said, Krissy would be better off going to a battered woman's shelter. Places like that had security systems. Places like that were equipped to handle situations like the one Krissy currently found herself in. Then Karen bid her niece good luck and asked her to stay in touch and hung up without offering Krissy so much as a dime to help her get back on her feet.

Krissy hung up the phone, trying not to curse her aunt in her head. *What would the neighbors think?* Angry, hurt and embarrassed, Krissy grabbed her purse from under the desk and pulled out her wallet. Tucked behind the latest Christmas picture of the girls was a carefully folded business card. Spence's business card. She had deliberately avoided calling him. She was afraid that he would catch hell at home if Chloe found out that the two of them were talking again. But Krissy was desperate. She unfolded the card and dialed Spence's work number. It rang and rang and rang. She was just about to hang up and try it again later that night when his voicemail clicked on.

She knew that Chloe would never agree to house her; she hadn't even been able to look Krissy in the eye when they'd seen each other in the restaurant months before. But Krissy hoped that maybe Spence could offer up a little emotional support and maybe even loan her a couple hundred bucks for lawyer money. She knew that waiting a year for a free or nearly free divorce was simply not an option, and mediation would be impossible. She at least needed to start thinking about paying for a lawyer and figuring out how she was going to get herself and the girls into a safe space.

Spence's voice was clear and strong and sounded so grown up. So professional. But he was still her little brother and it made her cry to think about how much time she'd lost with him. When she'd left her family to be with Dorian, he'd been a pimply faced teenager, but now he was a grown man with a family and a career and she had not been around for the transition from the one to the other. No matter what happened, she promised herself, she would never again walk away from her little brother.

Krissy left a message that she needed to talk to him right away. That was all that she said and hung up the phone after leaving her work number. She hadn't even strung her kitchen apron around her middle when Dan was telling her that she had a phone call and that she needed to make sure that she took it in the back office.

It was Spence. Krissy was surprised at how quickly he'd called back but also at how in control he seemed, even though he was well aware that something was very wrong. She explained why she needed to leave Dorian, what the lady at Legal Aid had said and what their Aunt Karen had said. She told him that all she really needed was to borrow a couple of hundred bucks to get her started and that she'd let him know as soon as she got settled at a shelter.

Spence said fuck that; she was gonna come and stay with him. He said that he was living in a rental out in Hamburg and that he and Chloe were in the process of getting divorced. He explained that Lenore was living with him, too, to help out with the kids. He told her that he would be there whenever she needed him, and that he would make sure that Lenore provided her with all of her lawyer money.

Krissy was overwhelmed. Just like that, it was going to happen? She was going to be out? Spence told her to call his cell phone from now on, and that if she was in immediate danger to call the cops and then to call him. Day or night, no matter the time, he would drive out and get her. In the meantime, he would speak to Lenore and they would bring the money to Krissy, probably within a couple of days. They would arrange to drop it with her at work and then she could figure out when she was leaving. He told Krissy to make sure that it was soon. He told her that he didn't want her living with that maniac for one more day. He told her that he loved her and that everything was going to be alright.

For some reason, Krissy believed him. Two days later Lenore and Spence stopped by the restaurant with eight hundred dollars in cash. Three days after that, Spence and Meagan pulled up to her apartment in their two mid-sized sedans and drove Krissy and her girls away.

Just like that.

Chapter 29

Marnie opened a beer before they'd even left the gas station parking lot and asked Krissy again if she was sure that she didn't want one, too. When Krissy shook her head no, Marnie took two long gulps before putting the remaining five beers on the floorboard next to Krissy's feet. "Hold mine, then," she said, handing Krissy the dark blue can.

They pulled back around the corner to Spencer's house and were about to head upstairs when Krissy remembered what was still in the trunk of her car. "I've got to get something. The ..."

"Oh, yeah," Marnie took another long sip from her beer can and followed Krissy to the back of the beat-up Celica. Krissy opened the trunk and the two women stared at the long black canvas duffel bag that held Dorian's mini-arsenal. "You gotta call the cops tonight," Marnie said, tapping a fingernail against the can like she was thinking. "We'll bring the bag in and leave it in the mudroom, O.K? I don't want it upstairs with the girls."

Krissy nodded her head in silent compliance even as she was reaching into the trunk and gingerly removing the lumpy bag. She handed the bag to Marnie, who immediately took it into the mudroom and placed it in a far corner before propping a couple of mesh lawn chairs in front of it. Krissy slammed the trunk shut and the two women walked back upstairs.

Marnie said goodbye and yelled for the twins. She told Lenore where the weapons were and told Krissy exactly what to tell the police when she called. She reminded Krissy that she needed to call soon, as it was getting dark outside.

Spence wasn't happy. "You left that shit in the mudroom? What if my neighbors see it?"

"It's all still in the black canvas duffel bag; how is that a problem?" Marnie asked, her face a mask of indifference.

"What if ... Jesus ... you know what? I'm gonna end up losing this place if people aren't more careful," Spence was trying not to look Marnie in the eye. "Whatever ..." he finally sighed, walking into the living room where Anna and Grace were still watching cartoons.

"Call the cops right now," Marnie whispered in Krissy's ear as she gave her one last hug goodbye, "before Spence has a coronary." She winked at her as if to signify that of course Krissy agreed with her that Spence was overreacting. Then she shouted for the twins again and was out the door in a flash, the two sullen preteens following silently behind her.

Krissy checked the sheets on Spencer's bed to make sure that they were reasonably clean, then changed the girls into their pajamas. She had always been meticulous about bathing them each and every night; just because they wore second hand clothes didn't mean that they had to look sloppy or unkempt. But that evening she simply pulled their nightgowns over their heads and washed their hands and brushed their teeth. She was too exhausted to even think about the rudiments of the bathing process. Wet and lather, scrub and rinse seemed as foreign and complex to her as physics. She just wanted them to go to sleep.

Krissy tucked them into bed and went to the kitchen and called the police. She told the dispatch attendant exactly what was going on; that she'd left her abusive husband and that she was living in hiding. She explained that the next day he was going to be served with a restraining order, but that she wanted to speak with an officer about securing some dangerous items she'd taken with her when she'd left her home. The lady said she'd notify the local patrol to stop at their convenience.

Krissy sat and watched television while she waited for the patrol car to show up. She thought about the inordinate amount of secular television the girls had been allowed to watch that day. She thought that if Dorian were there, he would yell at her and tell her that she was a lazy whore for allowing the television to babysit his two precious girls. But that was a silly thought, she chided herself, because if Dorian were there then she wouldn't be. If Dorian found her, she and the girls would have to go home. He would hold out his arms and Anna would fly into them and Grace would trail behind her sister and then he would have them. Then Krissy would have no choice but to bow her head and admit defeat and follow behind her husband. Back to the tiny apartment where he was the boss and only his thoughts and desires and wishes mattered. Where she was his whipping boy when he was angry or anxious. Where she represented to him everything that was wrong in the world and in his family and in his life. She would take the beatings and the name-calling and all of the screaming threats and horrible accusations and she would lower her head and let him do with her whatever he wanted, because she would never, ever, be able to leave again. He would never allow it. He would surely quit his job and stay home every day, all day, never taking his eyes off of his children, not even for a moment. She would never again have another chance like this one.

Spence was the first to notice the red, white and blue flashing lights bouncing off of the cars and houses that lined the short dead-end street. "What the ... Shit! The cop turned the lights on?! Is that really necessary? Jesus ..."

Krissy jumped up and Lenore tried to say something supportive as Krissy went flying past her. She was out of the apartment and down the steps in seconds, so she was breathless when she reached the mudroom.

It was pouring rain and cold outside, and the officer standing in the dim yellow glow of the porch light looked more than a little uncomfortable. "Ma'am, you called about needing assistance with some potentially dangerous items?"

Krissy opened the screen door and let him in, careful to look around him and out into the darkness before shutting the screen door behind him. Her nervousness didn't go unnoticed, and the officer turned his body so that he could look at her but still see out the screen door with his peripheral vision.

She told him just as quickly as she could what was going on, then pulled the lawn chairs back to reveal the duffel bag. She pulled the bag out and laid it on the floor between them, unzipping it so the officer might look inside. He scanned the bag's contents, unwrapping each item and giving everything a good once over.

"I'm afraid that if my husband finds me and this stuff is in the house, he'll use it against me," Krissy's voice was shaking, partially because she was cold but also because she was scared. The police officer had a funny look on his face that she couldn't read.

"Well, Ma'am, these items are your husband's property, correct?"

"Yes."

"When I take them with me, I'll be required to file a report and notify him that we have his property. The things that are illegal to possess in New York State will immediately be destroyed, but he has a legal right to have everything else back. Once he's notified, he'll have thirty days to retrieve the items. If he doesn't claim them, then they'll be destroyed, as well. "

Krissy was incredulous; she couldn't believe what the officer was telling her. "But what if he finds me? He'll try and kill me, *with this stuff*!"

"I understand your concerns, Ma'am," the officer explained, though he was starting to look annoyed, "but it's the law."

"Fine," Krissy said, leaning down and zipping the bag closed, "then I'm not giving them to you."

She was close to tears and exhausted and had had just about as much as she thought she could take for one day. "You know, I could have thrown all this stuff into the river! I could have pitched it into a dumpster or just thrown it all out the car window on some back road when we were driving out here!" Krissy could hear her voice raising, but it sounded like someone else's voice and she was interested to hear what else that very angry woman was about to say. "But I didn't! I wanted to do the responsible thing! I wanted to make sure that some kid didn't get his hands on this shit and hurt himself or somebody else with it!" Krissy could feel hot tears beginning to sting the corners of her eyes.

"Alright Ma'am, just calm down."

Krissy apologized. She thought that the officer still looked annoyed, but there was something else there, too. Something in his tired eyes that told her he was trying to figure something out; that he was thinking.

Thinking, thinking, thinking.

"Look, this is what I can do ..." The officer told Krissy that he was going to need to take the stun baton and the Billy club; they were illegal to possess in New York State and now that he'd seen them, he was obligated to confiscate them. Then he paused, and when he spoke again his voice was low and serious and he held Krissy's gaze in a deliberate stare. He told her that since she was married, all of the property that she'd removed from her home was technically hers, as well as her husband's. He told her that it was also technically her right to keep everything else in the duffel bag, though if she wanted to, she could choose to surrender to him the SAP gloves and the pepper spray. Then she would have to sign a statement detailing all of the things that she was surrendering to the police to be destroyed.

He also told her that since everything she was surrendering was technically considered joint marital property, if Dorian called to inquire about some things that had gone missing from his home when his wife left him, the police were legally obligated to tell him that they had his things and that he would be able to retrieve the items if he chose to. If he didn't call to claim them, then all of the items would be destroyed after thirty days; that was how long the police had to hold them. After thirty days, both she and her husband would receive notices in the mail detailing what items of theirs had been surrendered and informing them that all of the items had been destroyed.

Krissy breathed a sigh of relief. She wanted to hug the police officer but didn't.

He quickly wrote down all of her information and Dorian's information and she reminded him that she didn't want Dorian to know where she and the girls were. She told him again about the order of protection, mentioning that her lawyer had told her it would most likely be valid for ninety days. He noted that in his small scratch book and Krissy hoped that he wouldn't forget and accidentally list her brother's address on the notification to Dorian when it was mailed out in thirty days. Then she handed the officer the duffel bag. He fished through it and removed the gas masks. They were harmless, he told her, shaking his head in what Krissy thought looked like disbelief.

He went back to his patrol car and Krissy waited there on the damp, dimly lit porch for what seemed like forever. When he came back, he had paperwork for her to sign. Then he told her to be careful; to watch her surroundings whenever she was coming in and out of the house. He told her that if there were any problems with her ex-husband that she should call the police immediately. Krissy asked how often patrol cars came around, and the officer said about once every hour. Krissy asked what she should do if Dorian came to the door. The officer said that if he came anywhere near her at any time that she should immediately call 911. But, he impressed upon her before he left, there was only so much that the police could do, and that it was primarily up to her to be aware of her surroundings in order to keep herself and her children safe.

The rain started coming down even harder as the officer said goodbye and walked to his patrol car. Krissy watched him turn onto Maple Road and drive away. Cottage Way was dark and quiet again, save for the one street lamp on the corner. She looked around one last time and shivered, wondering what was next.

She went upstairs and tossed the gas masks into a large black garbage bag that she found under the kitchen sink. Then she checked on the girls, who were still awake. She tucked the garbage bag into the farthest corner of Spence's narrow bedroom closet before plopping down on the bed between the girls and reading to them from one of their storybooks. When Anna asked if they were really going to be living with Grandma Lee and Uncle Spencer for a while, Krissy said yes, but that very soon the three of them would be getting their own apartment and that Grandma Lee and Uncle Spencer would be able to come and visit them there. Anna asked if Daddy was going to come and live in the new apartment with them. Krissy said no, that Daddy was going to stay in their other apartment. Anna said O.K. and Grace just laid there listening, and Krissy kissed them both good-night and told them she'd be in to sleep with them later.

She closed the bedroom door and she and Spence chatted for a few minutes before he left to go to Meagan's for the night. Lenore peeked her head into the living room as Spence was hugging Krissy goodbye and asked if there was anything Krissy needed before she turned in for the night. Krissy said no, that she was fine. Lenore said she loved her, but didn't offer a hug or a kiss and Krissy was thankful for that. Krissy turned off the TV when she heard Lenore's bedroom door latch.

The apartment was dark except for a dim light over the stove. Krissy was starting to feel anxious, even with the fatigue of the day weighing heavily on her. The words of the officer rang in her head. It was up to her to be aware and alert. It was up to her to keep herself and her children safe. She turned around and peeked over the back of the short leather couch and out onto the street where the Celica sat. The moon and the street light shone on the white car, making it look to Krissy like a beacon in the night. Dorian would recognize the car immediately if he happened to drive by. Krissy kneeled up over the back of the couch and rested her chin on her arms. What if he found her? How would she keep him out? He would pound the door down for sure in order to get to his girls.

Her legs were tired, too tired to continue kneeling into the soft bulk of the couch. Krissy crawled up and sat on the couch's cold, smooth back, her shoulder pressed up against the window frame. She tried to position herself so that in the darkness, no one would be able to see her sitting there.

Her heart raced and her throat was tight and she was sure, oh so sure, that Dorian was going to pull up at any moment. In whose car, she had no idea, but she knew her husband; he was not a man who was easily deterred. And when it came to his daughters, she knew that Dorian would find a way.

Or maybe he wouldn't pull right up. Maybe he would park around the corner and walk up. Silently. Stealthily. She watched like a scared jackrabbit as she reached behind her and pulled at the orange crocheted afghan that sat on one arm of the couch, flipping it this way and that until it covered her now outstretched legs. She watched the street and the car and the mudroom door and she waited and prayed and cried.

Please, God; please don't let him find me.

Leaving Dorian

Several times that night Krissy woke with a start. Once she got up to pee, but otherwise she stayed perched in that window well all night long. Lenore found her the next morning, face pressed into the window glass, her body cold and stiff and her neck sore. She stroked her daughter's cheek lightly and whispered for Krissy to wake up. "Have you been here all night?" Lenore asked. She had tears in her eyes and a look on her face that Krissy wanted to label as compassion. Krissy nodded her head and started to pry her stiff, sore body out of the window well.

"I'm going to make some coffee and breakfast. Do the girls like pancakes?" Lenore asked, heading back toward the kitchen. Krissy said yes and Lenore said good, that she'd make some sausage links, too.

Krissy looked out the window. The river flowed silently by and contractors were already driving up and down Route 5 and the neighbor was putting his dog out and her car was still sitting where it had been every time she'd awoken during the night to look for it. It was undisturbed, as was the mudroom door.

Dorian had not found them.

He was not all powerful and he was not all knowing and though he was probably sitting all alone in their old apartment plotting and scheming a way to find her, he hadn't that night.

Krissy slid down the back of the couch and stared at the closed bedroom door that she knew her daughters were sleeping peacefully behind. For the first time, she thought that there was a very good chance that she was going to be able to do it. To stay gone. To not be Dorian's wife anymore. Because she'd done something that she hadn't imagined was possible; she'd made it through one whole day and one whole night without him. And so had the girls.

No great punishment had come down from Heaven to smite her for her iniquity, and the girls certainly hadn't fallen apart under the weight of a day full of junk food and TV and strangers. Nope, the girls had gotten through it just fine. And so had she.

Krissy rubbed her eyes and yawned and realized that she felt hopeful. What lay ahead? She had no idea. But whatever happened, she knew that she'd manage, because nothing could ever be as bad as living with Dorian. And now she knew that she didn't have to.

Linda Dynel

Appendix

Please be aware that while each of the resources listed below can be accessed electronically, all devices can be monitored (ie, computer, tablet, phone, etc.) and it is impossible to completely clear a device's search history. Please seriously consider your personal safety before accessing any of the following agencies on your personal device; public libraries have computers that are free to use and Internet ready.

National Coalition Against Domestic Violence
ncadv.org

National Domestic Violence Hotline
1-800-799-SAFE (7233)
Text "START" to 88788
ndvh.org

National Sexual Assault Hotline
Chat: online.rainn.org
1-800-656-HOPE (4673)
rainn.org

FaithTrust Institute
faithtrustinstitute.org

Muslim Women's League
mwlusa.org

Christian Survivors/5 Petals Project
www.christiansurvivors.com

Linda Dynel

The following was written in October, 2023:

"I am a difficult woman. There is no doubt about this. There was a time in my life when I wasn't. I spent decades being accommodating. Compliant. Polite. Palatable. I had been taught growing up to be user-friendly. Demure. Charming. Consumable. I was raised by my grandfather. He was the kind of man who said things like, "She wouldn't say shit if she had a mouthful". He liked that about me. I was a living embodiment of his belief system; everything that my mother had refused to be. He would tote me out in front of his friends and they would smile and he would smile and everyone would agree: I was pretty. I was sweet. I was worthy.

After being married to a man that nearly killed me (twice) and another who spent nearly two decades using me to suit his needs, I've evolved into a woman who deliberately and with aforethought goes against the grain of patriarchy. In taking a stand and refusing to bend, I've learned that opposing those in control makes you unpopular. To that I say: good. I no longer wish to be tolerated by the majority. I also don't care about being liked, especially by those whose value systems I do not share.

There were years sandwiched in between demure and difficult that I tried mightily to be neutral, though once you see something, you cannot unsee it. Educating myself on the topics of intimate partner violence, sexual abuse and assault, men and masculinities and feminism are what opened my eyes. The books that I read on those subjects were like cobblestones, paving my way from compliant to resolute. Every work that sits on my bookshelf today helped to transform me from a young woman desperately looking for acceptance, to a middle-aged woman who would rather burn her life to the ground a third time than sit quietly and comply. Education changed the way that I move through the world. It was a catalyst in changing my marital status. It changed the way that I parented both of my daughters, and my son. Ultimately, the education that I availed myself in my adulthood changed everything.

This is not an easy way to live. Choosing sides has also affected me professionally. I have readers and students who love my work, but are left cold after hearing me speak. Taking sides is now what I do best, though, and there is no going back. I will continue to evolve. There can be no change without growth, and there is never growth without learning. I am excited to embark on the remainder of my life's journey, wherever that may take me."

<u>NOTES</u>

Made in the USA
Middletown, DE
30 August 2024

60058683R00117